PATTERN MOTIFS

PATTERN MOTIFS

A SOURCEBOOK

GRAHAM LESLIE McCALLUM

BATSFORD

First published in the United Kingdom in 2006 by
Batsford
10 Southcombe Street
London
W14 0RA

An imprint of Anova Books Company Ltd

ISBN 9780713490237

A CIP catalogue record for this book is available from the British Library.

15 14 13 12 11 10 09 08 07
10 9 8 7 6 5 4 3 2

Reproduction by Classicscan, Singapore
Printed and bound by SNP Leefung Ltd, China.

This book can be ordered direct from the publisher at the website:
www.anovabooks.com, or try your local bookshop.

Distributed in the United States and Canada by Sterling Publishing Co.,
387 Park Avenue South, New York, NY 10016, USA

DEDICATION

To my two Saluki hounds, Sirocco and Shikari, my constant companions
during the many lonely hours it took creating this book.

ACKNOWLEDGEMENTS

The Master Designer.
The artists and craftsmen of the past.
Razien Samuels, Norma McCallum, Charlene Weber and Nadine Foord
for their assistance and encouragement.
The Durban Municipal Library and the Durban Reference Library.

CONTENTS

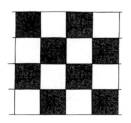

INTRODUCTION

If we were to take a single motif, even the most simple of motifs – for example, a black dot – and then placed several similar dots together, evenly spaced along an imaginary line, we will have created a linear pattern. There is something visually pleasing in this most basic pattern – not only beautiful, but psychologically satisfying too. Extend that collection of dots vertically and you have amplified the pleasure effect.

This is precisely what our ancestors did 30,000 years ago. These cave-dwelling men and women discovered this aesthetic effect, carved this pattern onto their bone implements and painted it onto the walls of their rock shelters. Here we are, in the 21st century, still appreciating that very same pattern – only now, we call it the polka-dot pattern.

That you have picked up this book and taken the time to page through the patterns and motifs is proof that you have an appreciation for patterning. Many scholars have theorized endlessly about the reason for mankind's fascination with design, but like most of our desires and passions, the reasons lie deeply buried and locked away within our complex psyche. However, I would like to think that, as you explore these wonderfully decorative pages, you unlock that mystery and discover the secret to your personal passion for decoration.

In truth, the creative mind is not the only source for decorative patterns; the natural world has pipped us to the post, producing some of the most beautiful and varied delights. Even our very finger and palm prints are nature's unique patterns imprinted on our hands. Taking a closer look at several wonderfully decorative tropical shells or the fascinating pelts of wild animals is a humbling experience. Indeed, you'd find it tremendously difficult to improve on nature's originality.

Fortunately for us, thousands of talented artists and craftspeople have preceded us and left an extraordinary wealth of motifs and patterns. The cultural creativity of the past not only provides a generous source of design and decoration, but also a wealth of motivating inspiration. It is like unlocking a chest and finding it brimming with jewels and finely wrought treasures in gold and silver.

Within these pages, I have catalogued the many arrangements that we find pleasing, from mankind's earliest Stone Age attempts, right through to the modern Art Deco style. This volume contains many types of patterns; the chequered, the stellar, the scale-like, the spiralled, the arabesque, and many, many more. Some of these decorative styles were championed by different cultures and at different times. Greek design is a fine lesson in restrained styling using a set number of design models, while the Gothic style is a good instructor of creative exuberance and the Japanese style a tutorial in simplicity.

These special and distinctive designs have been taken from many sources. Some are from the age-old pottery of the Neolithic period – so bold and assertive in their dark brushstrokes. Others are from the intriguing jewellery of the Egyptian dynasties, like those golden and enamelled treasures discovered in the tomb of the Pharaoh Tutankhamen. Yet others were collected from the exquisite images painted on the walls of Minoan palaces. The mosaics of the Byzantines, the architectural friezes of Romanesque cathedrals and the maze-like relief work on Chinese bronzes were the source for many more. This wide field of motif and pattern sourcing affords the user of this book numerous and varied applications.

In this age of digital cameras, personal computers, graphic software and colour printers it is easy and quick to take a snap-shot of a flower in a garden and print out as many images of it as you would wish for. Why is it then, that with all these electronic aids at our disposal we still find the simple patterns and motifs, made up of basic shapes, lines and forms and executed by hand, to be more satisfying? Here lies the crux of the mystery and the value of this book: we have a compelling drive to manipulate, extrapolate, redesign and re-interpret nature. We are not content to simply photograph natural images for our decorative purposes, rather, we desire to leave the mark of our hands and to reveal our thought-processes for all to see and appreciate.

This book caters for this well-defined, enduring and classic creative tradition. Something of the life force, the movement of the designer's hand, the passion, even the very soul of the artist, is forever captured in these motifs and patterns. Fortunately, for those of you who want to simply capture a pattern for a project from this fine tradition, modern copying methods are quick and effective. All the artwork has been executed in fine and exacting detail for your visual enjoyment, for your inspiration and to assist you in your many creative pursuits. The black and white images in this publication facilitates their accurate reproduction. The line-drawn images make hand-reproduction much easier. Many of the complex patterns have accompanying registration marks to help the user locate the beginning, midpoint and ending of pattern sequences. The reference dots indicate the scale to which the patterns were drawn and therefore will help with grid and hand-copying. Please note that you may only copy or adapt designs for your personal use.

I am certain that within this book's rich heritage, you will find the style, the look and the type of motif and pattern that you are searching for to complete all your projects and I trust that the many beautiful images will be the key to unlocking and releasing your own innate creativity.

Graham Leslie McCallum

STONE AGE EUROPE

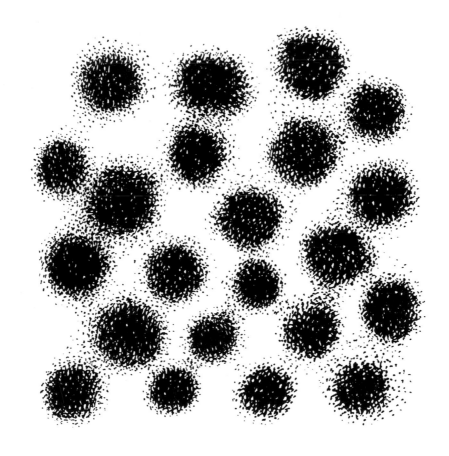

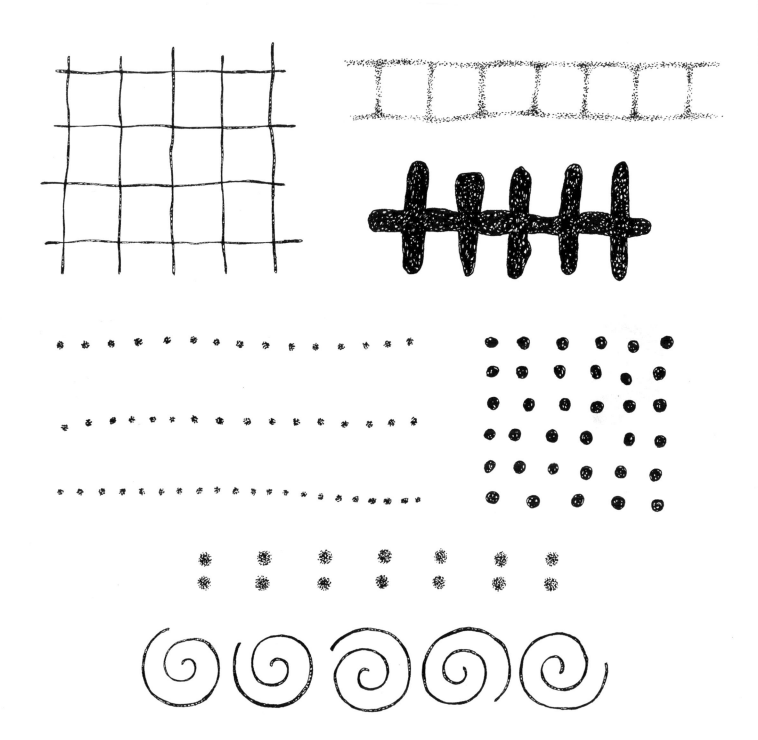

NEOLITHIC EUROPE

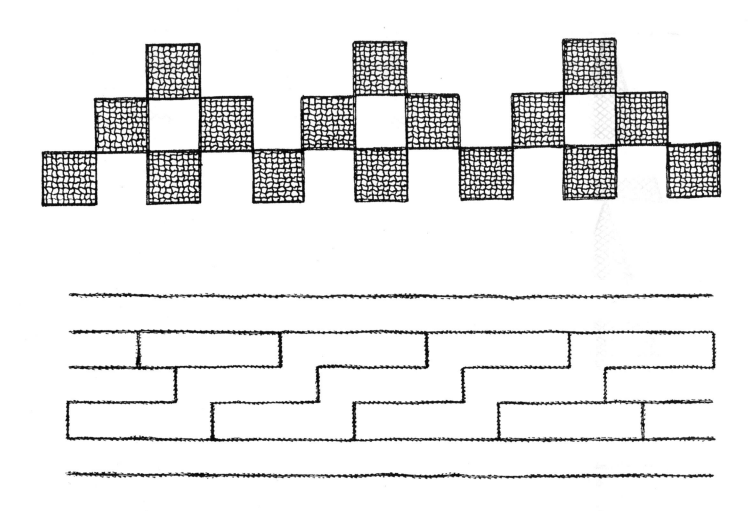

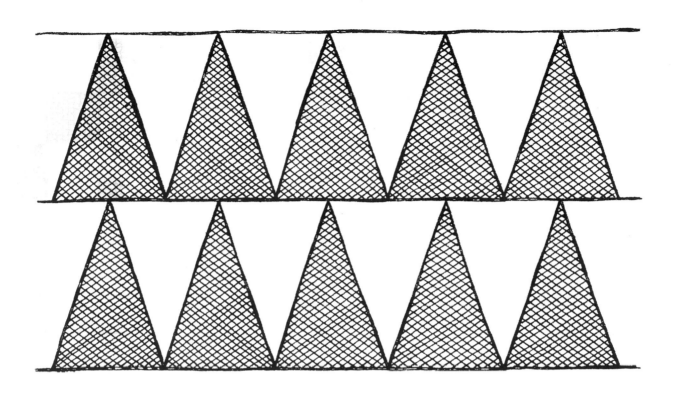

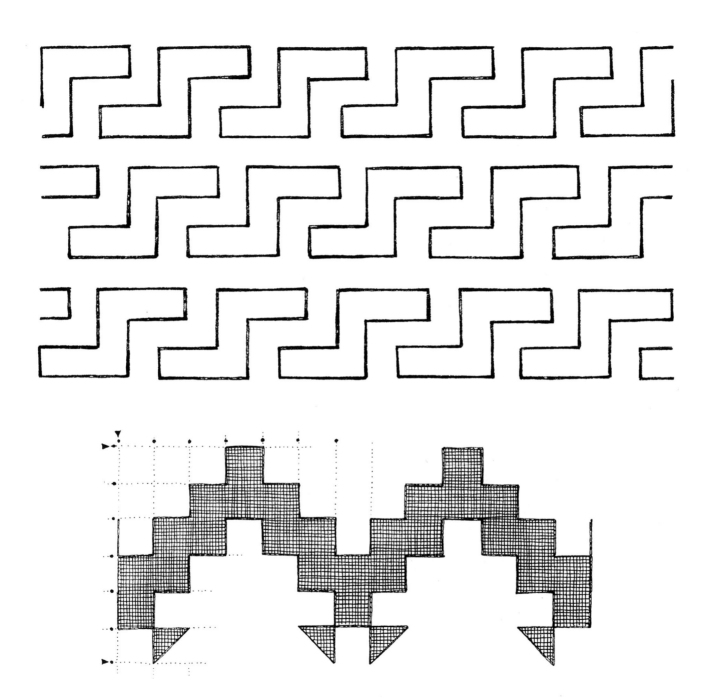

MESOPOTAMIA

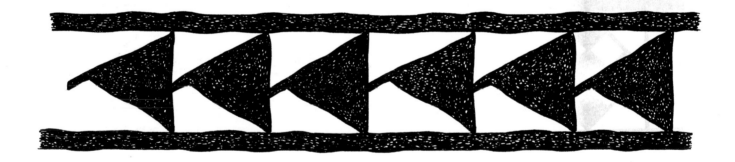

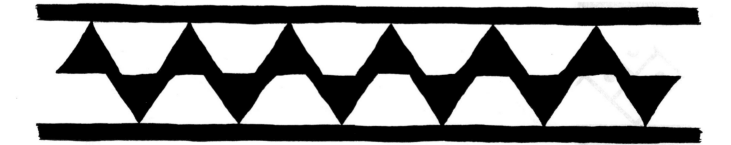

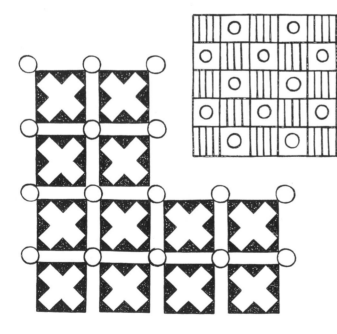

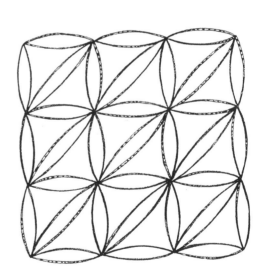

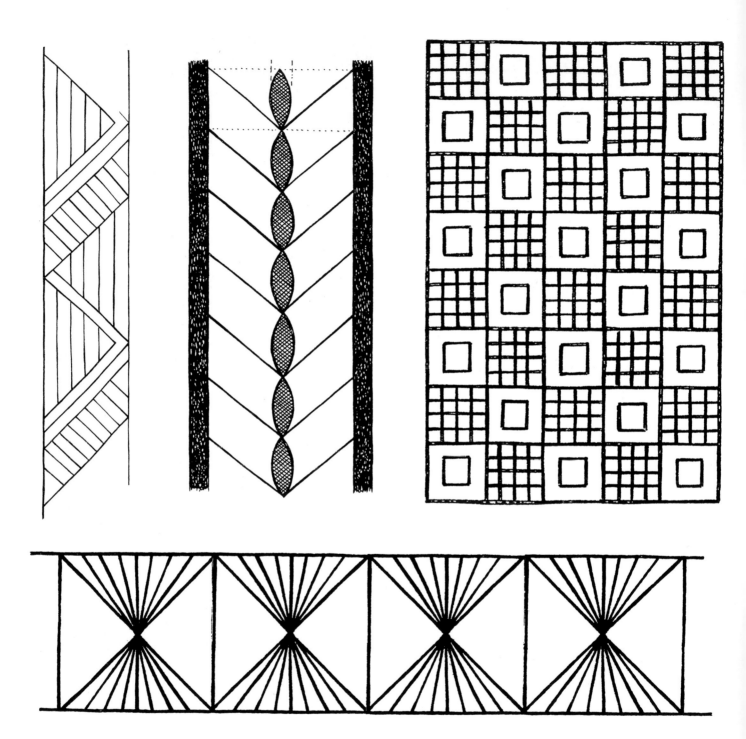

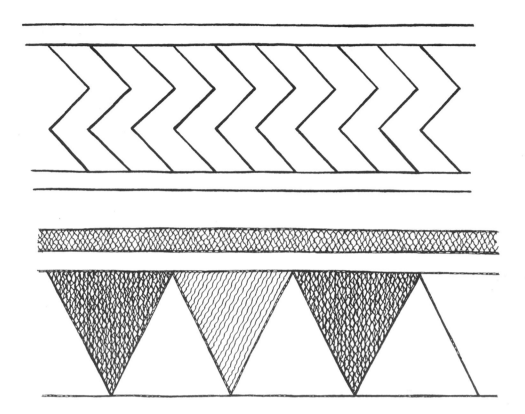

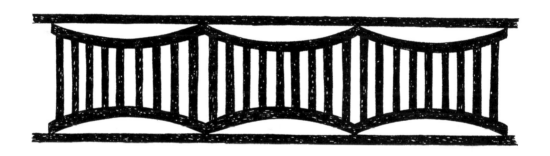

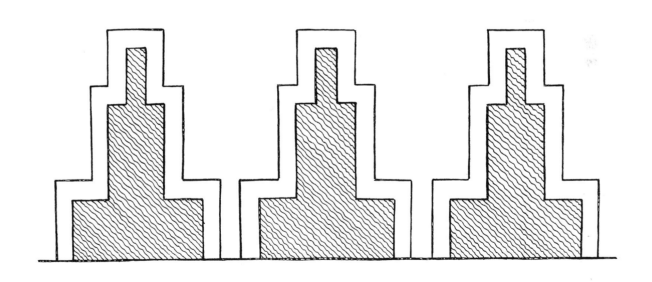

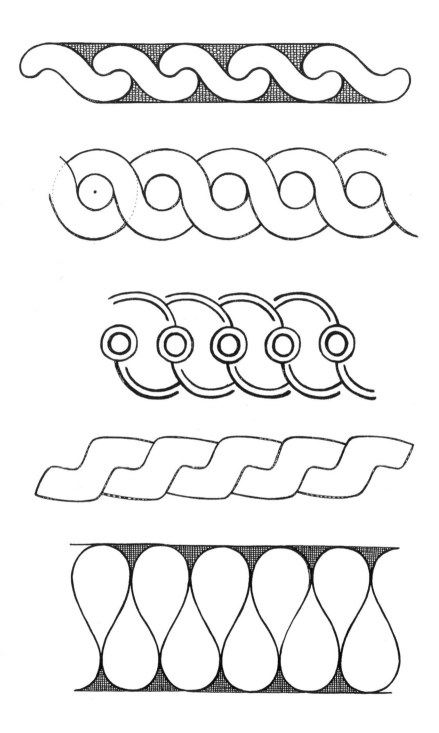
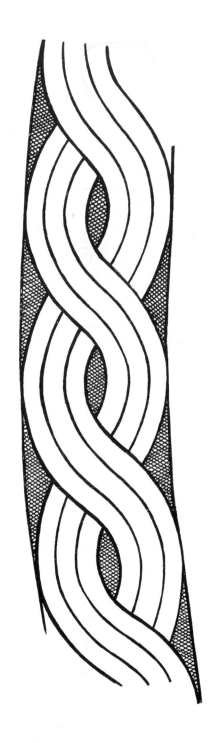

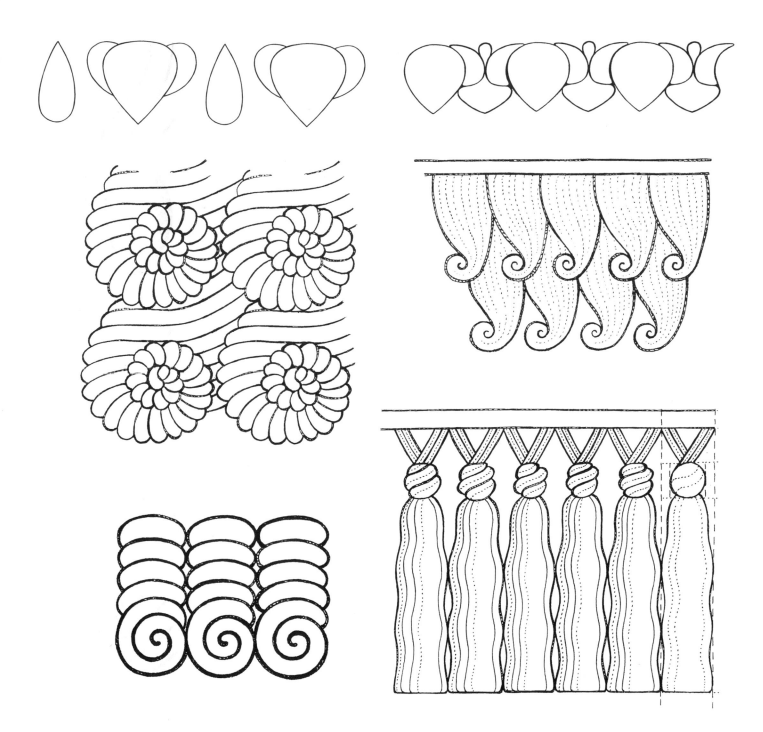

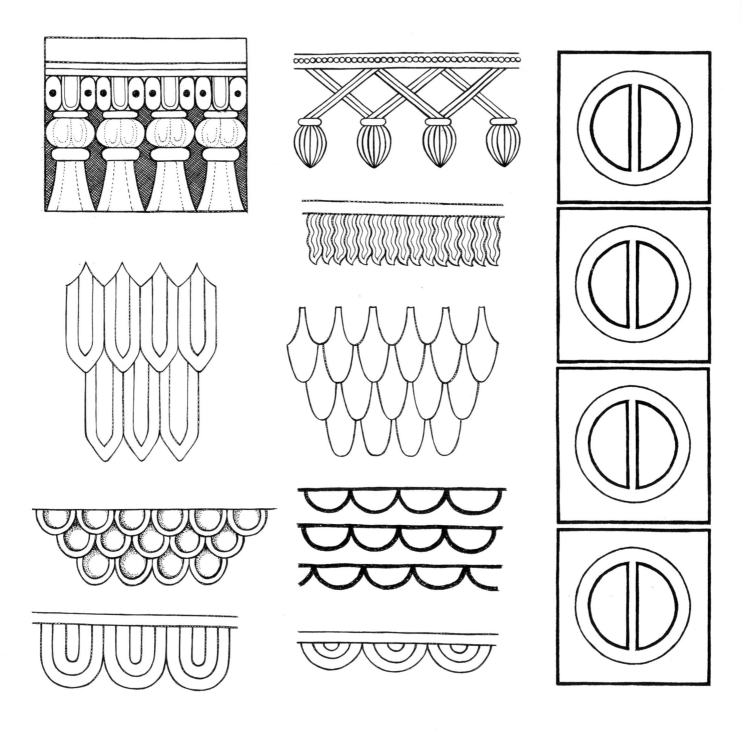

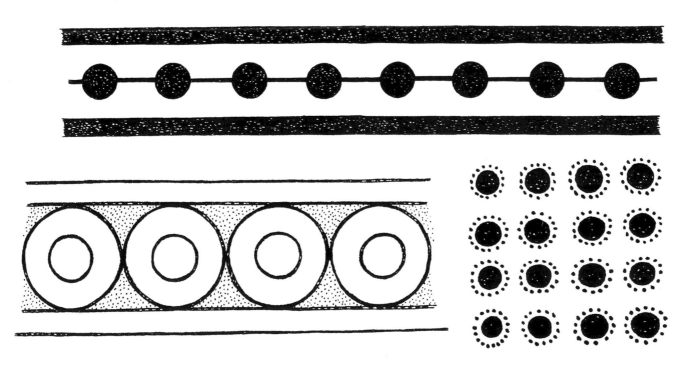

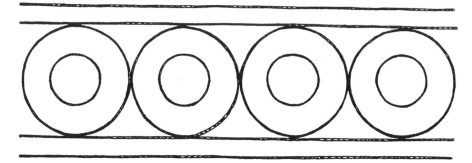

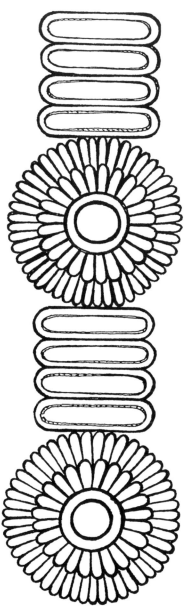

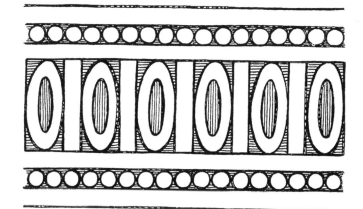

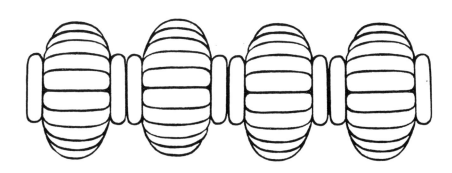

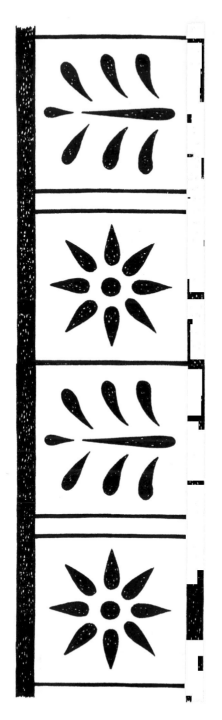

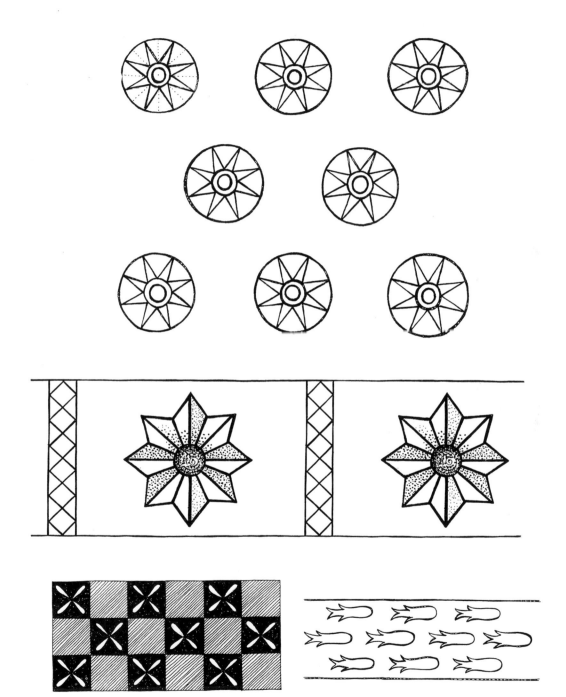

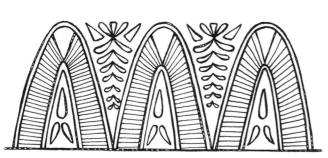

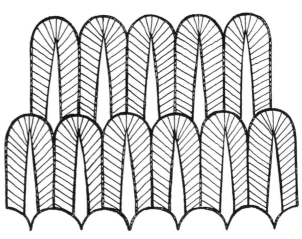

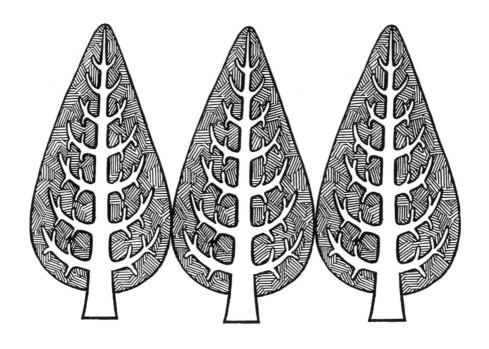

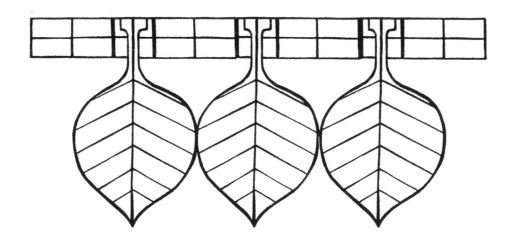

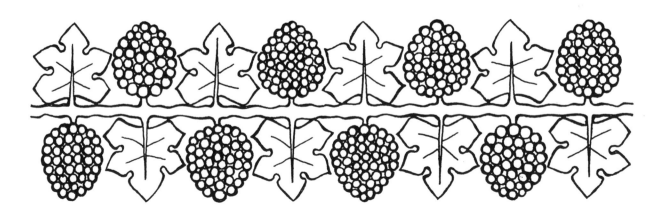

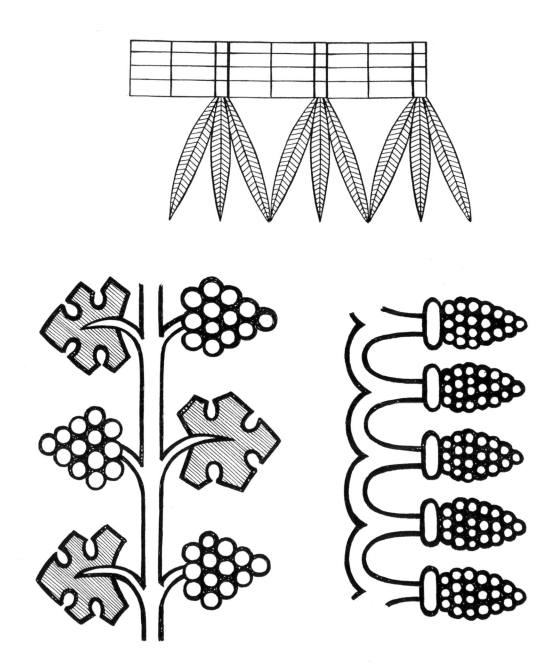

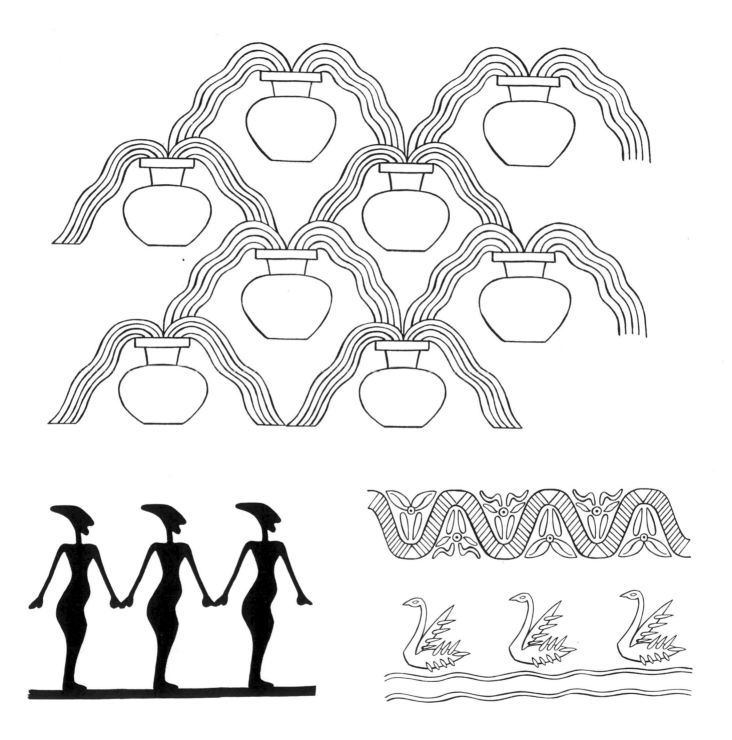

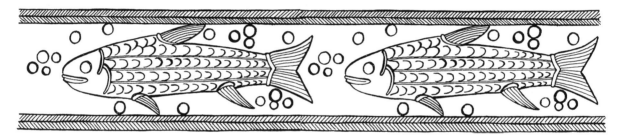

EGYPTIAN

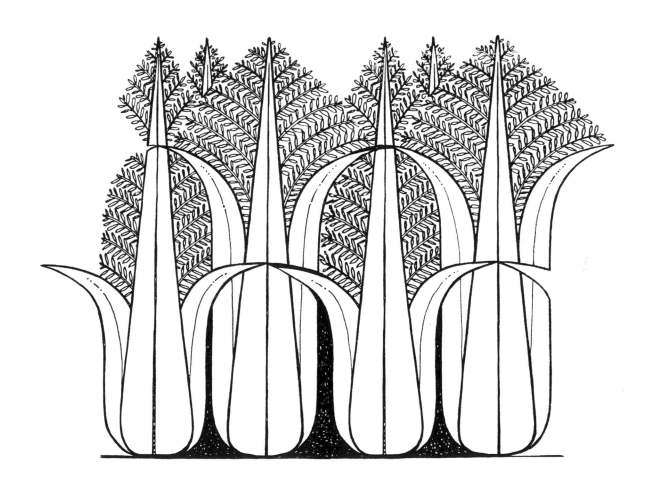

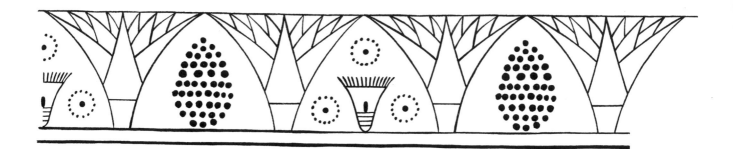

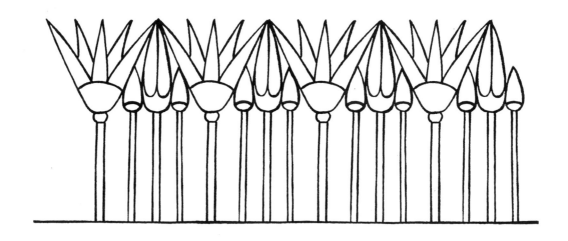

66 EGYPTIAN

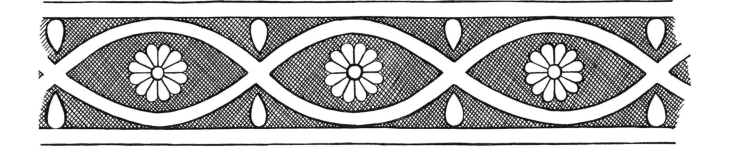

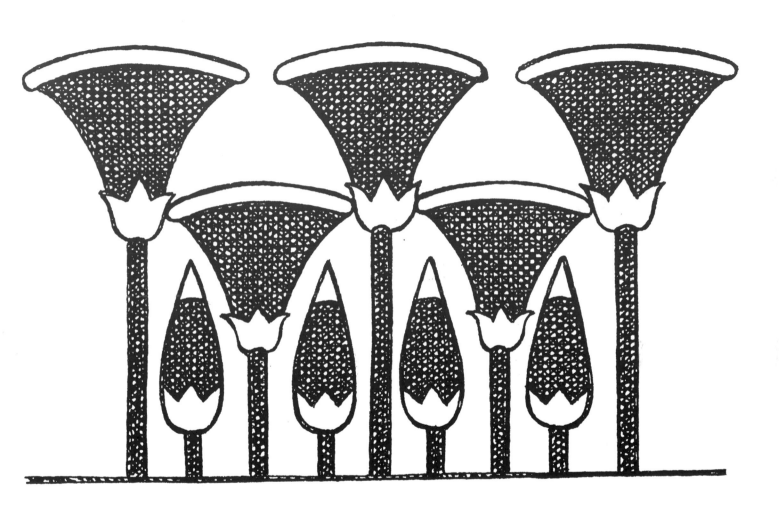

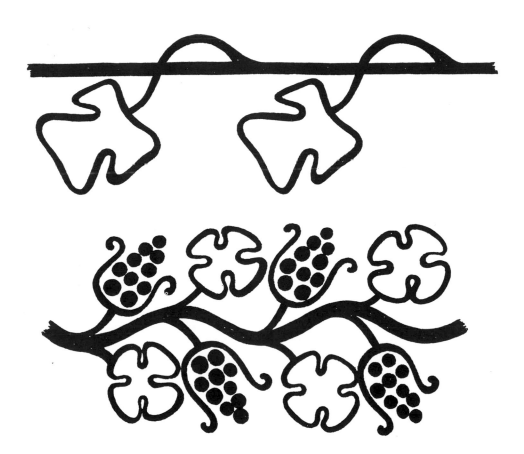

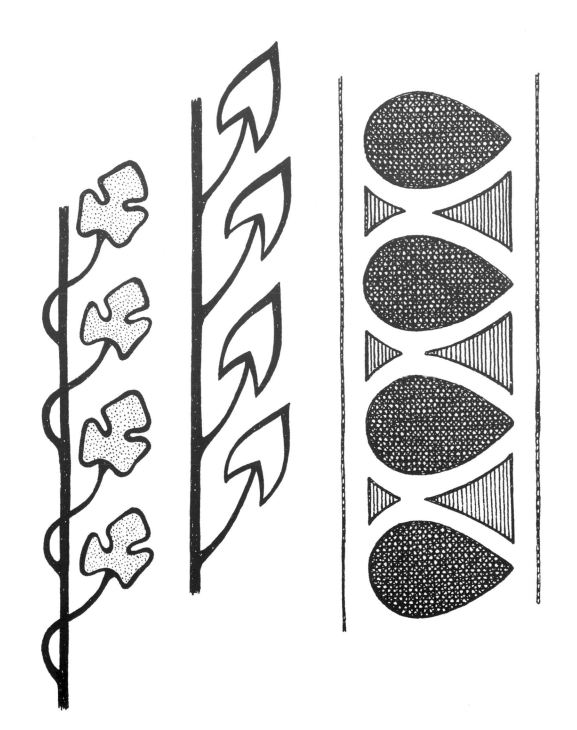

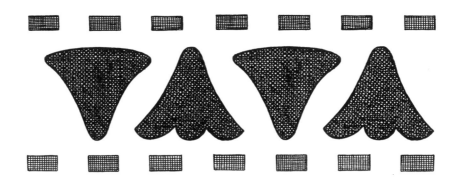

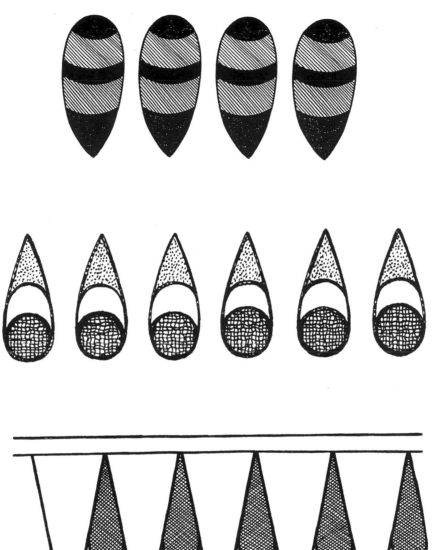

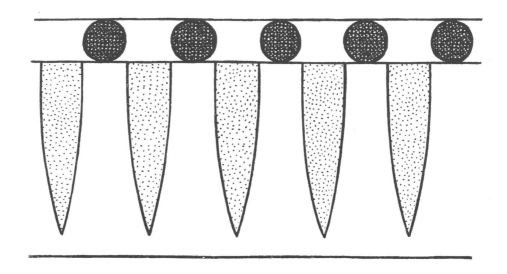

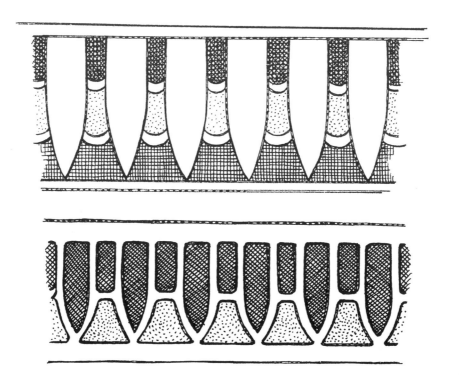

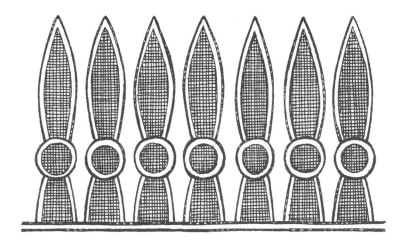

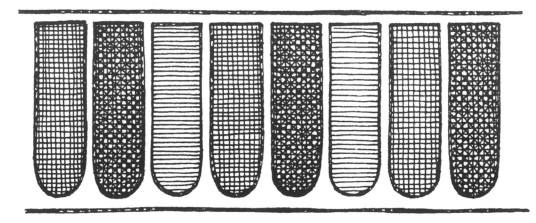

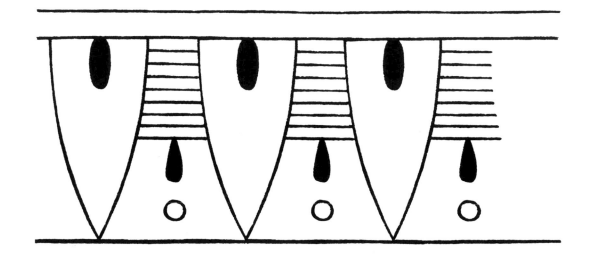

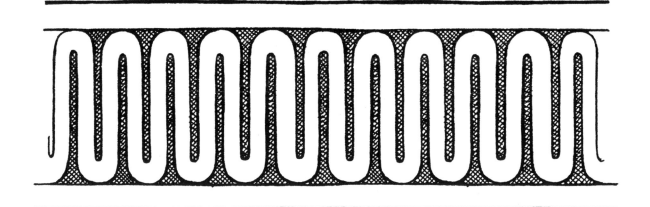

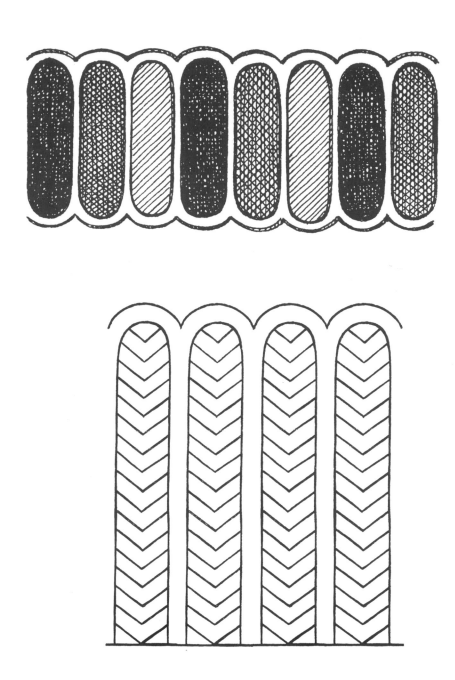

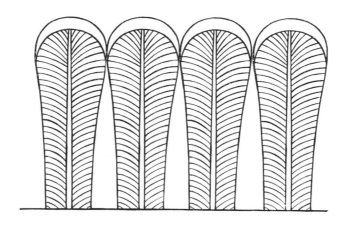

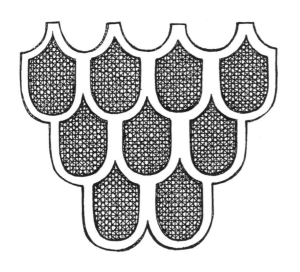

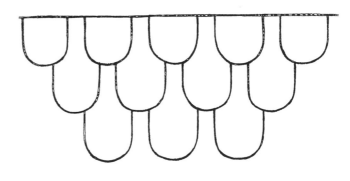

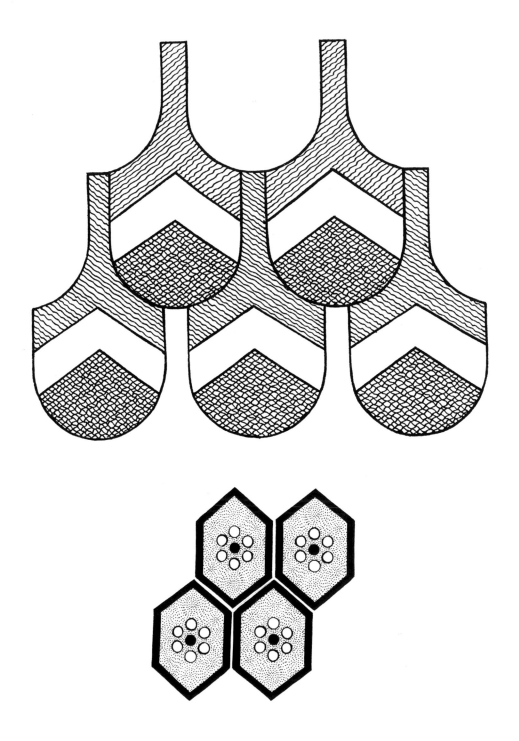

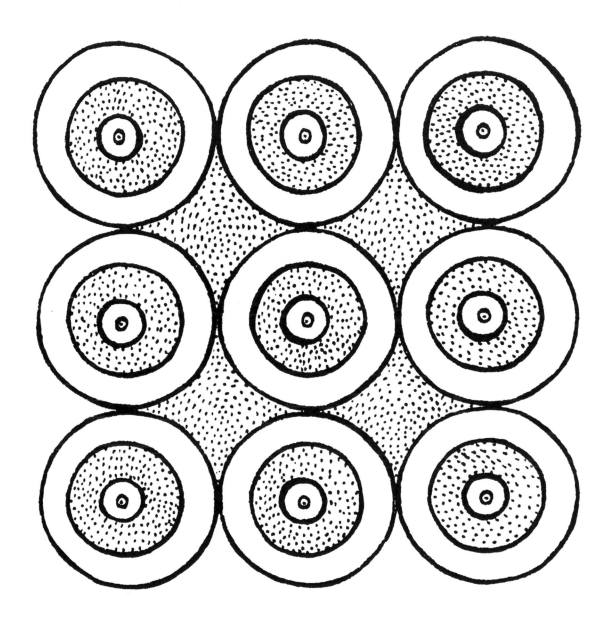

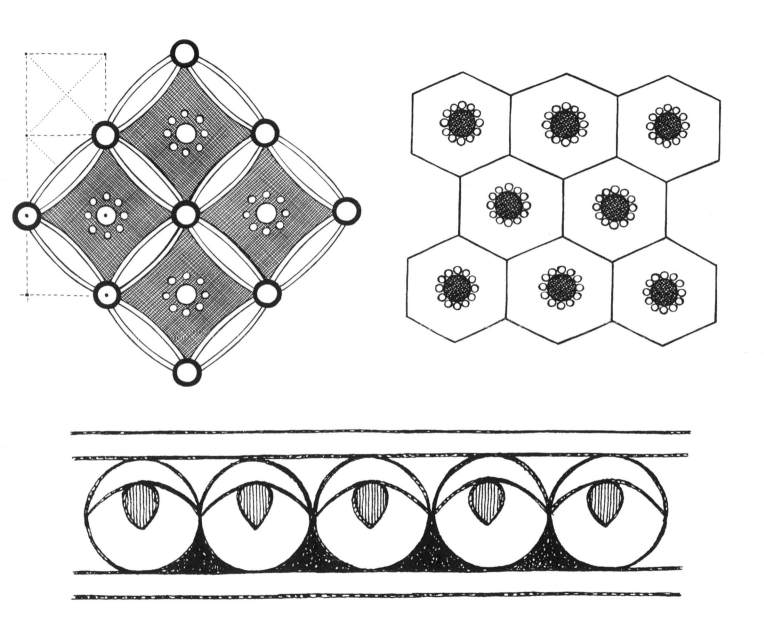

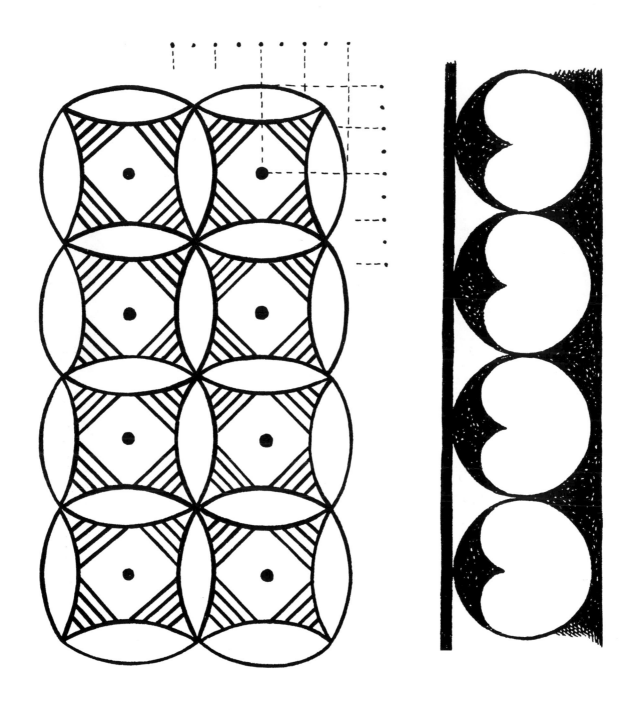

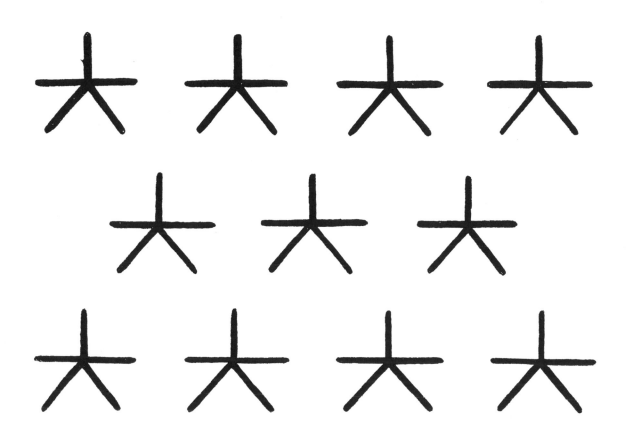

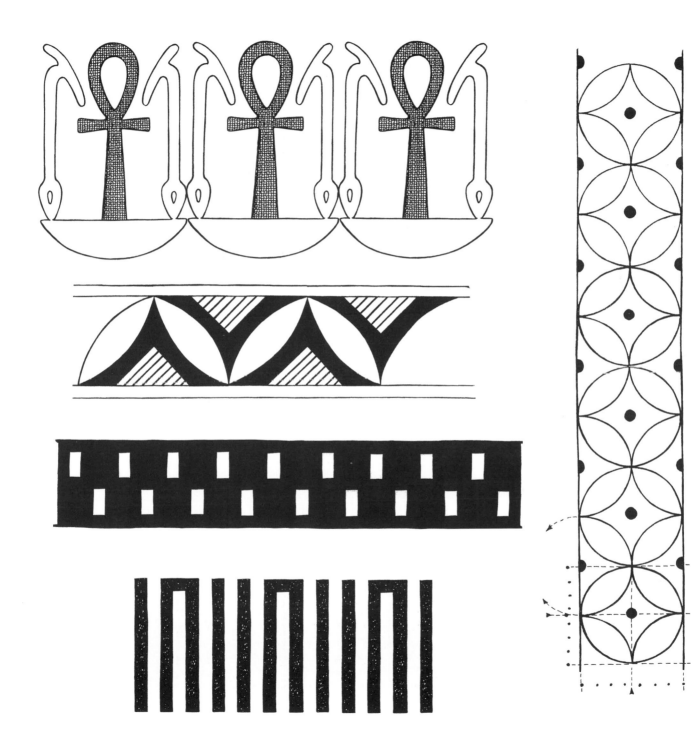

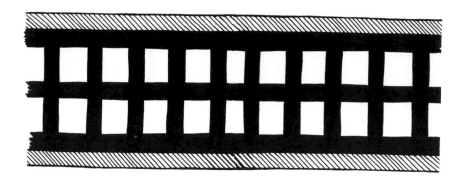

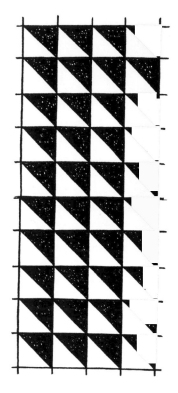

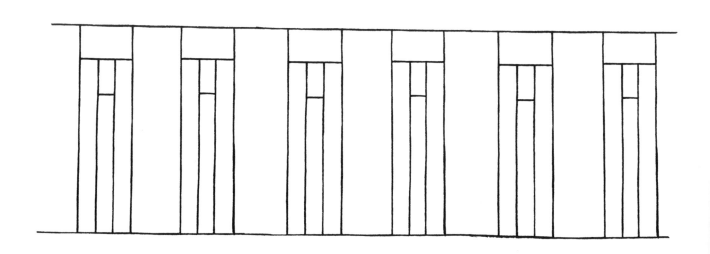

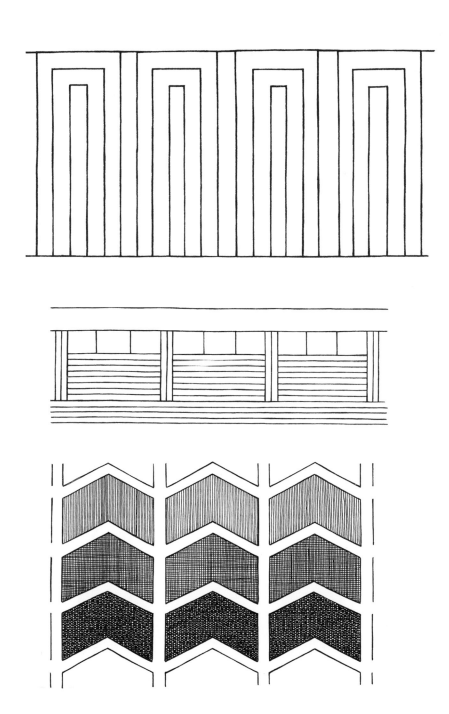

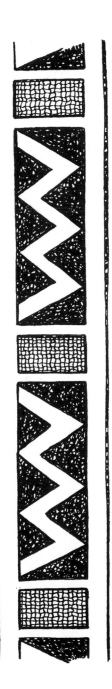

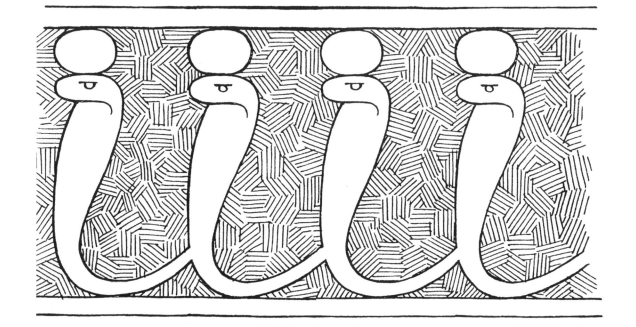

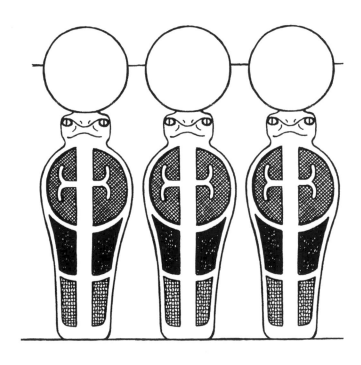

MINOAN

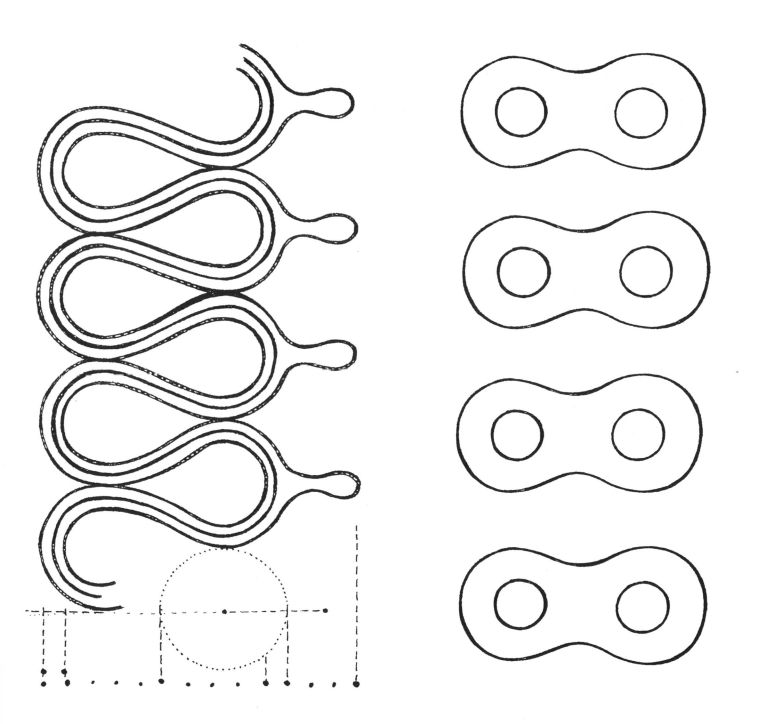

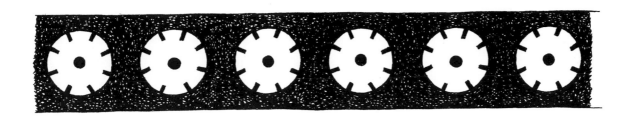

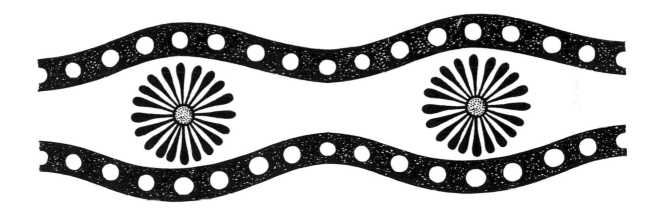

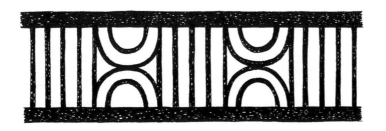

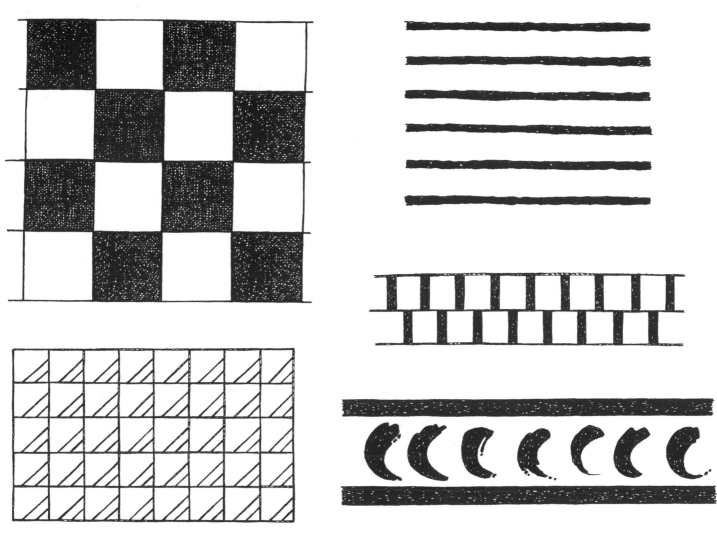

MYCENAEAN

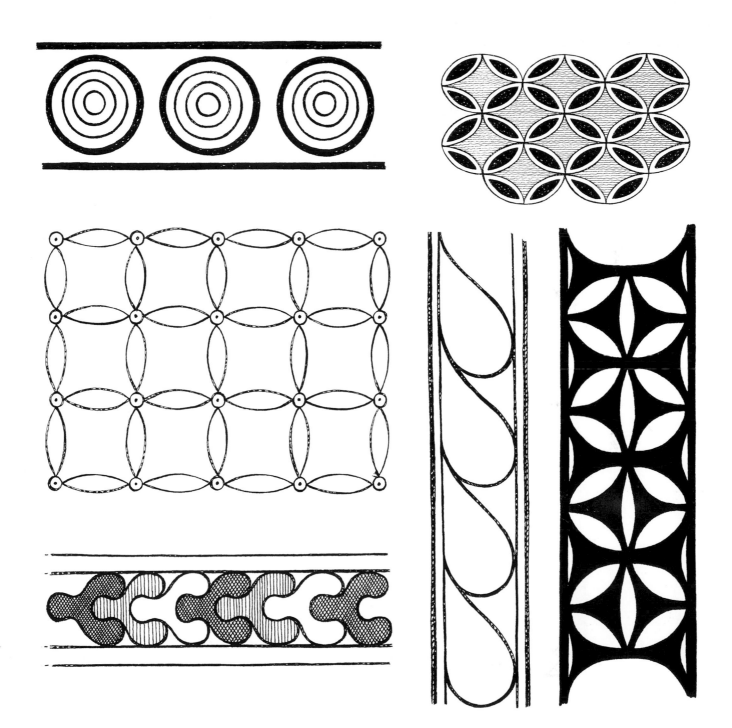

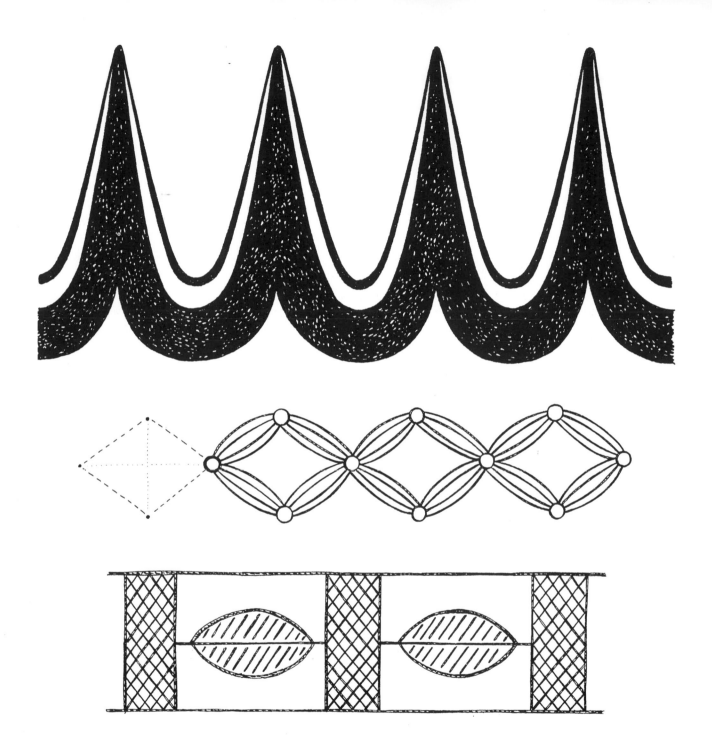

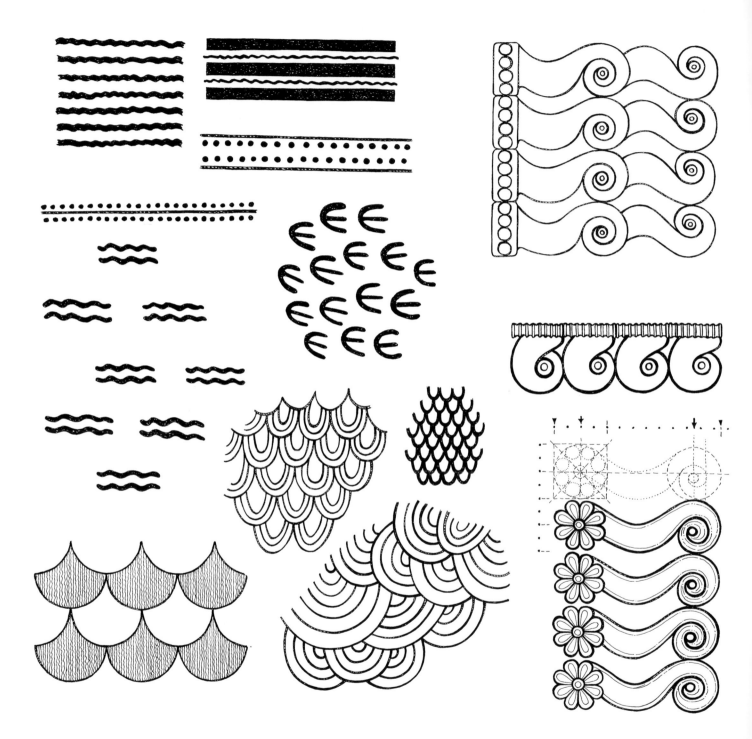

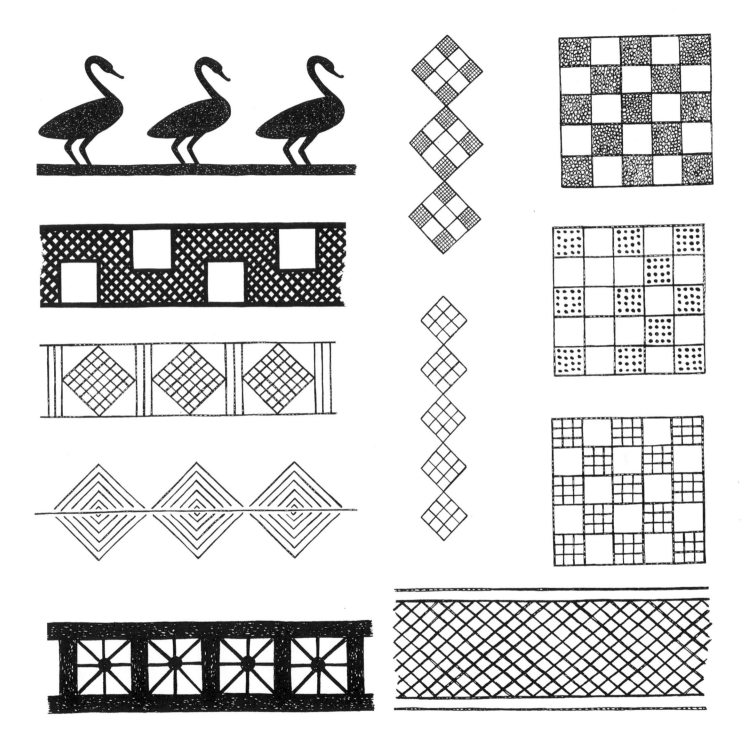

GREEK

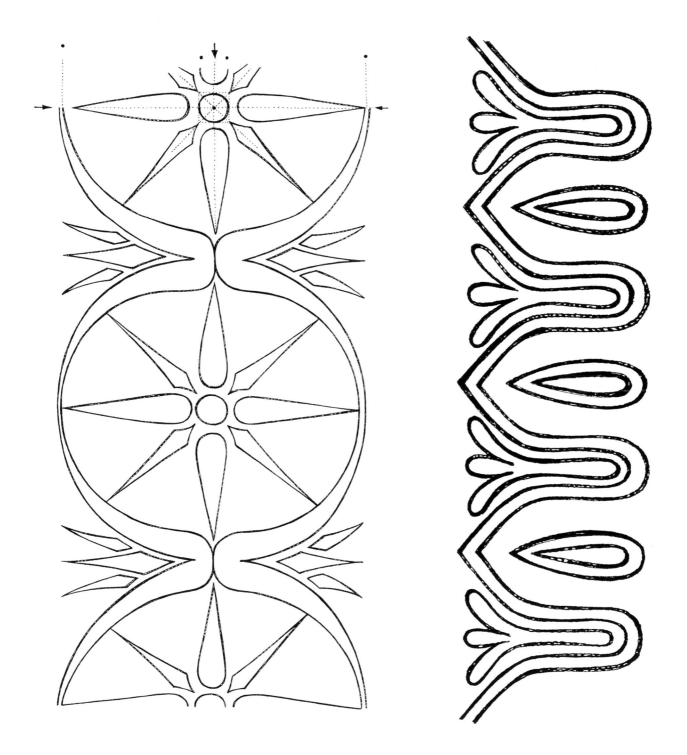

132 GREEK

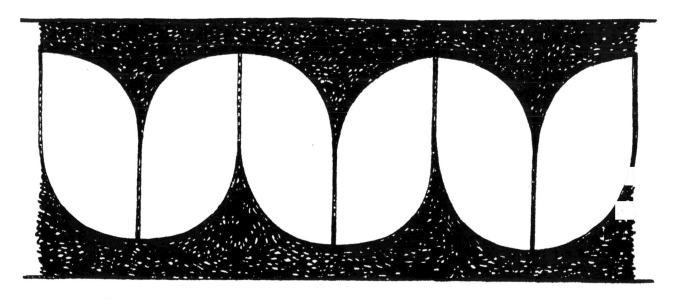

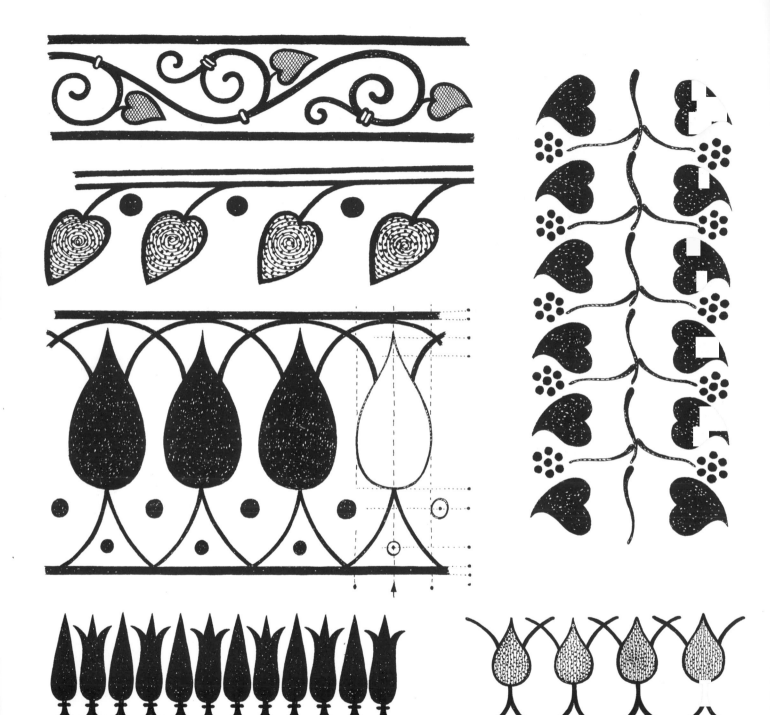

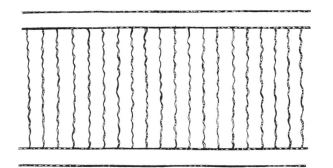

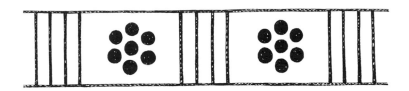

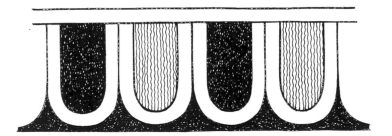

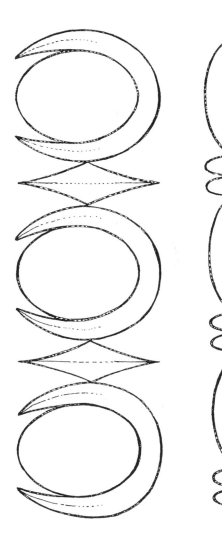

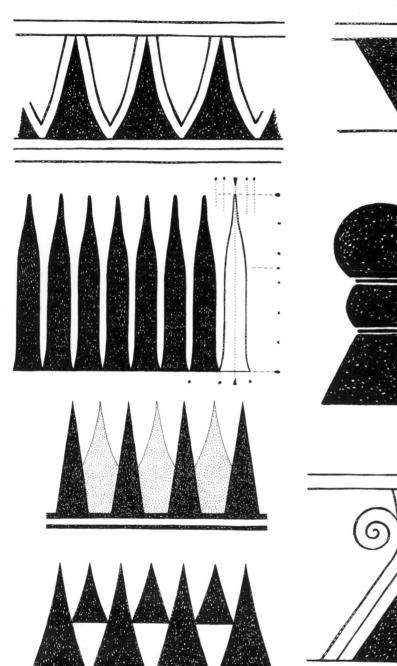

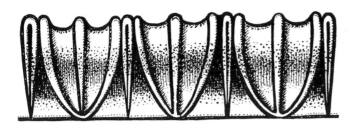

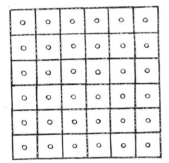
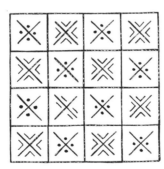

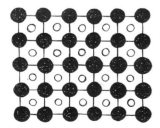
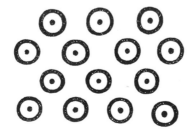
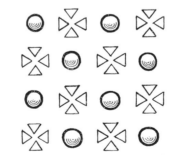
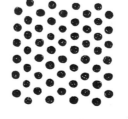
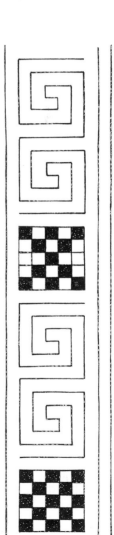

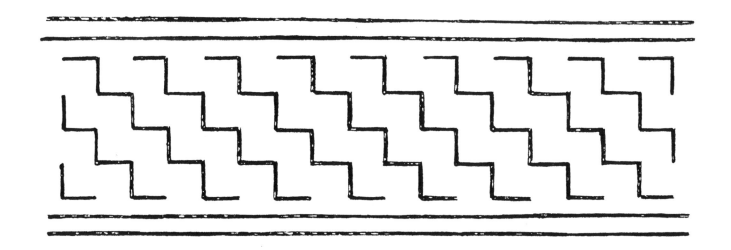

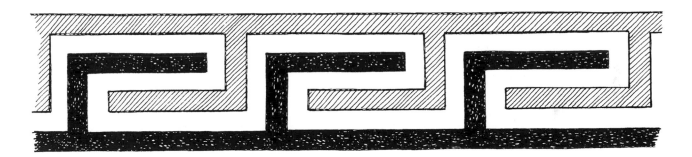

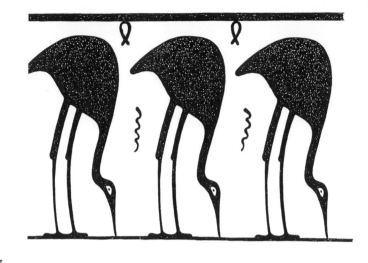

CHINESE

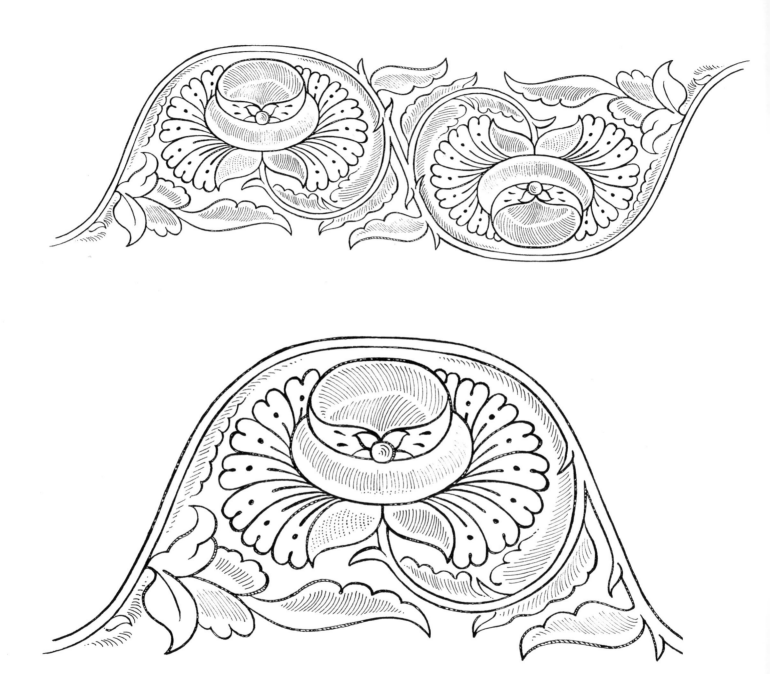

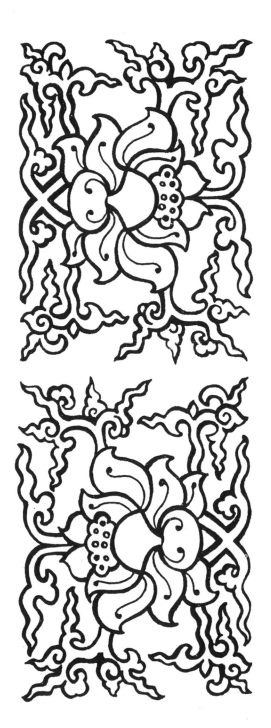

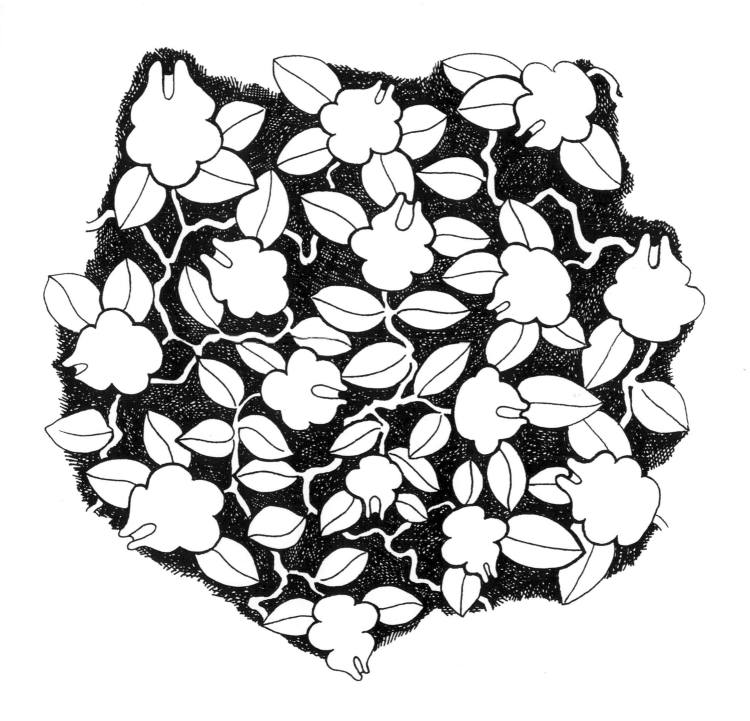

160 CHINESE

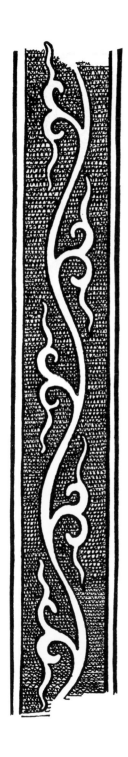

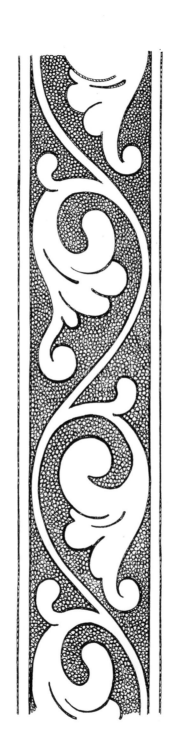

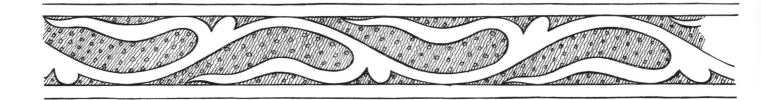

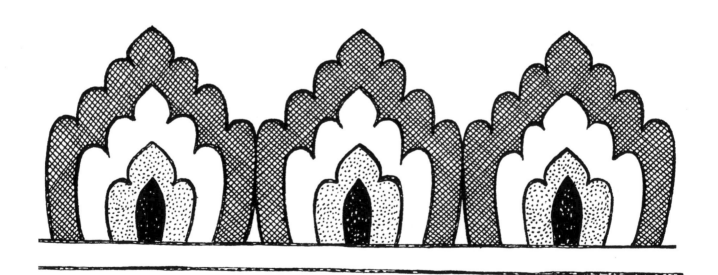

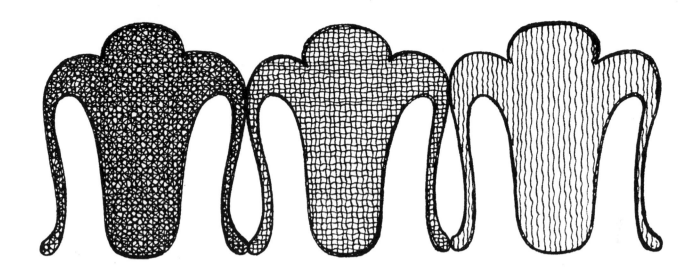

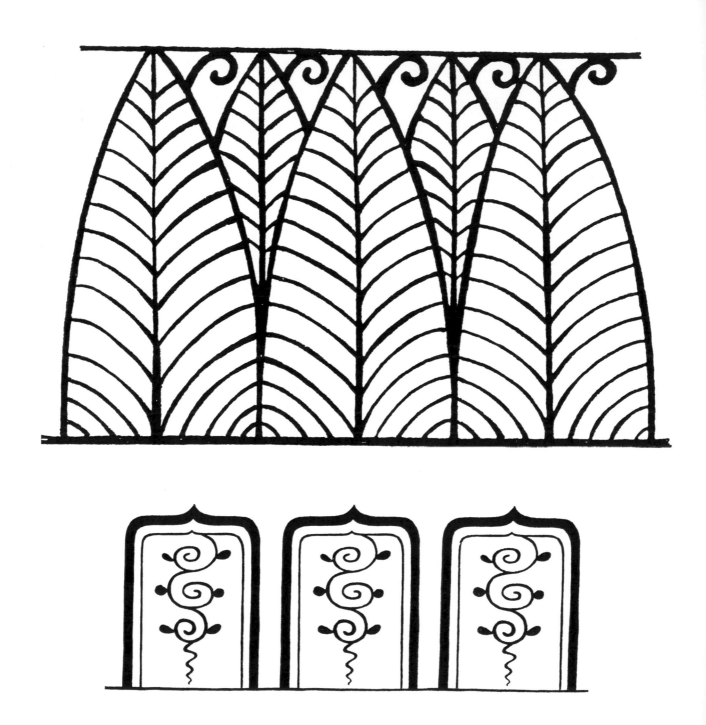

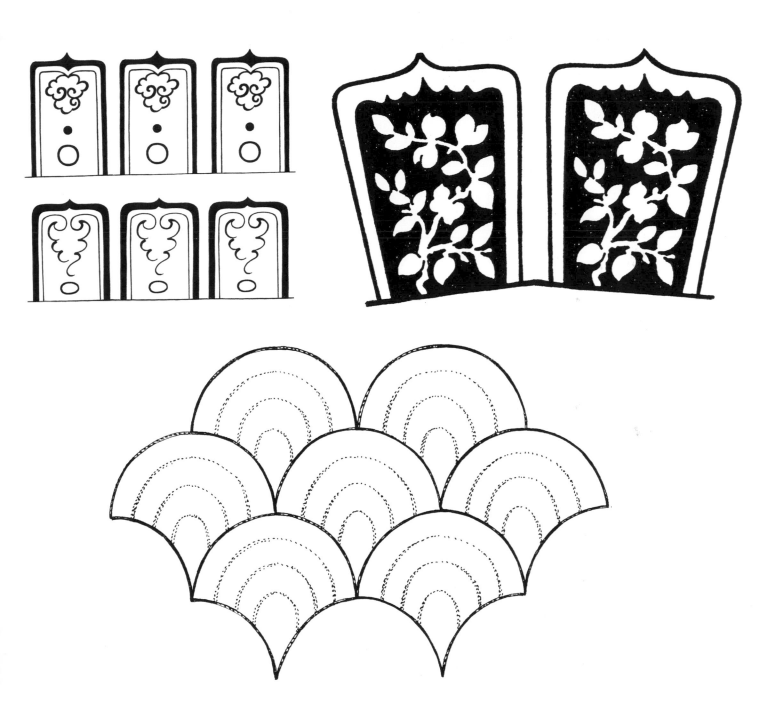

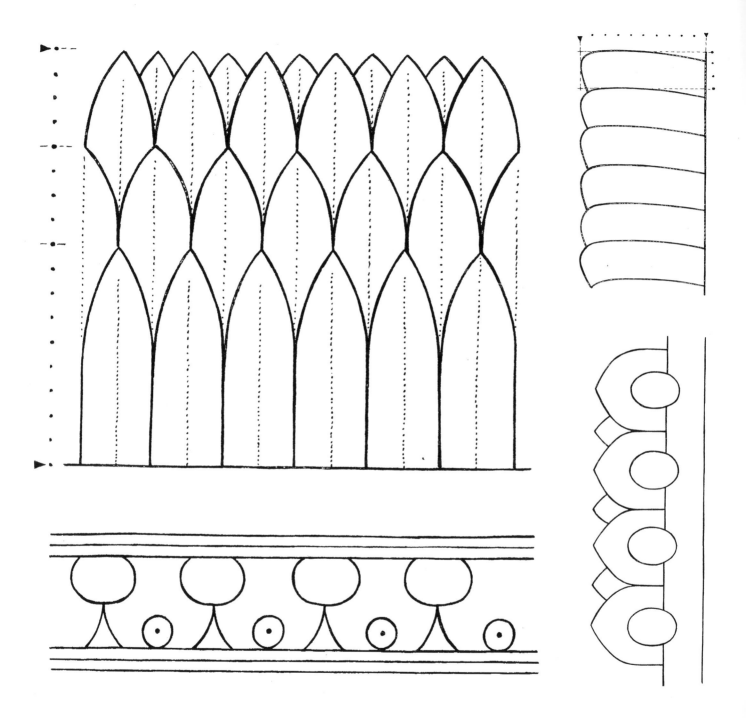

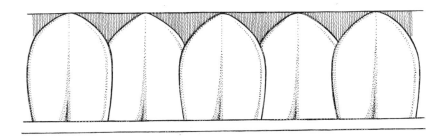

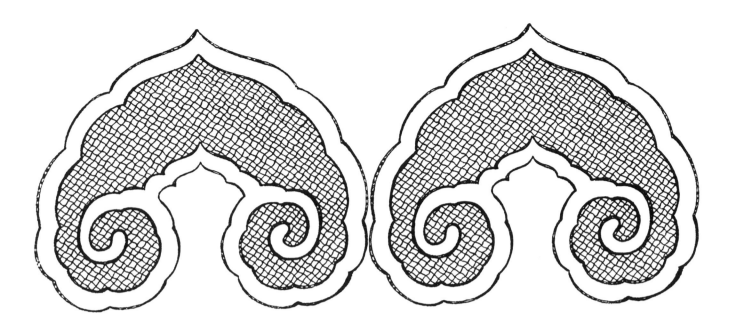

EARLY CELTIC

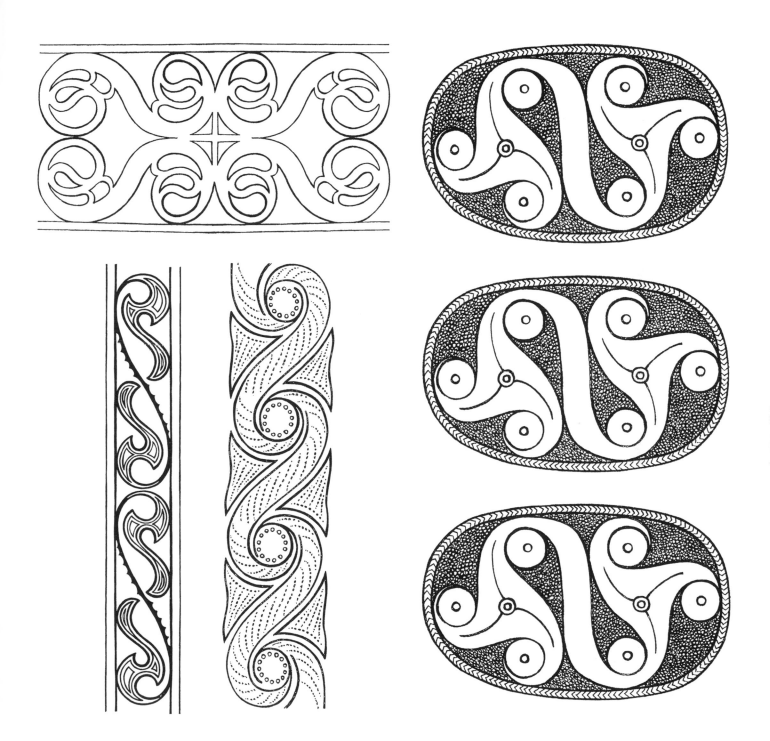

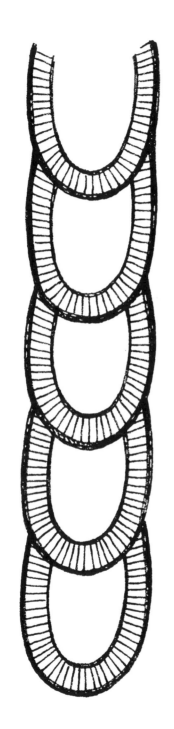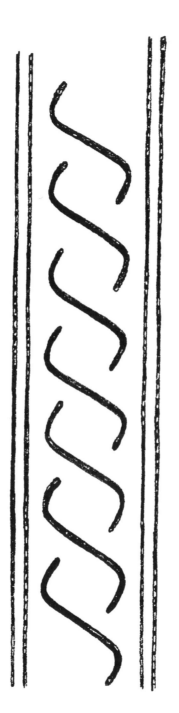

186 EARLY CELTIC

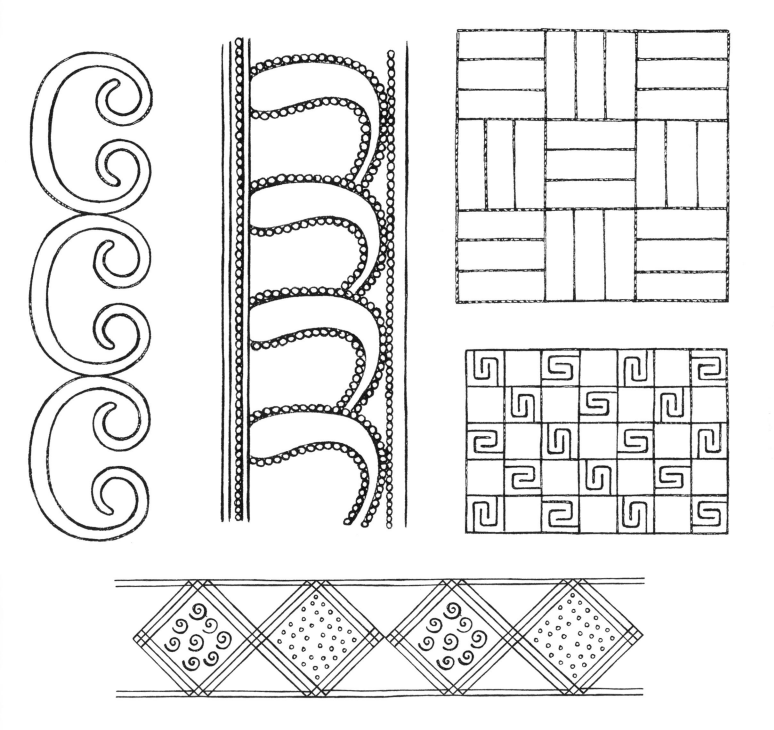

BARBARIAN

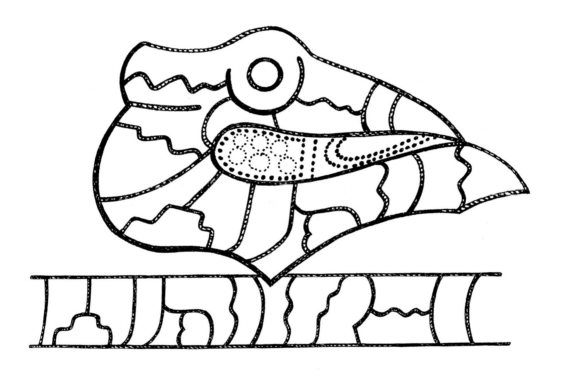

196 BARBARIAN

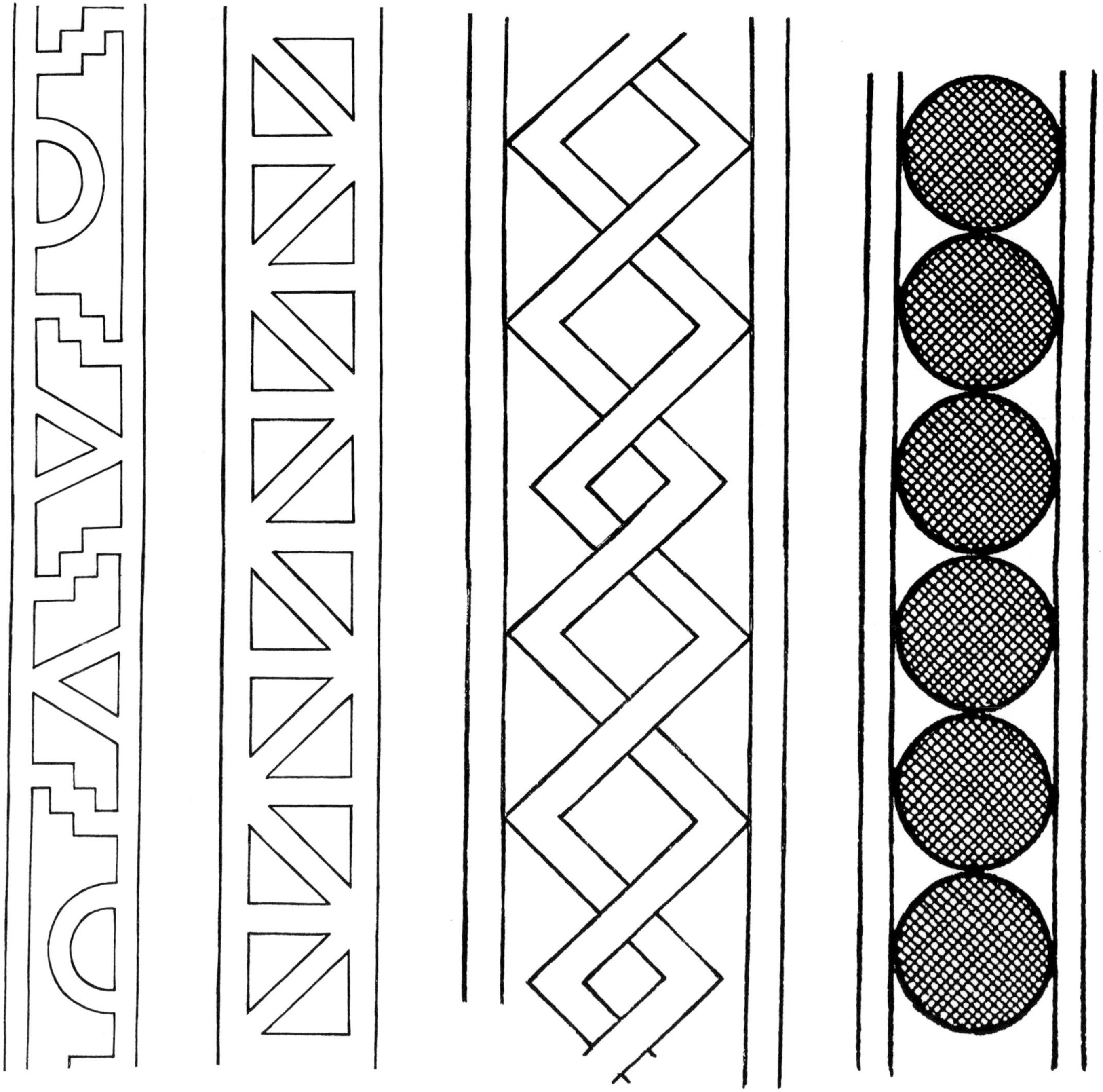

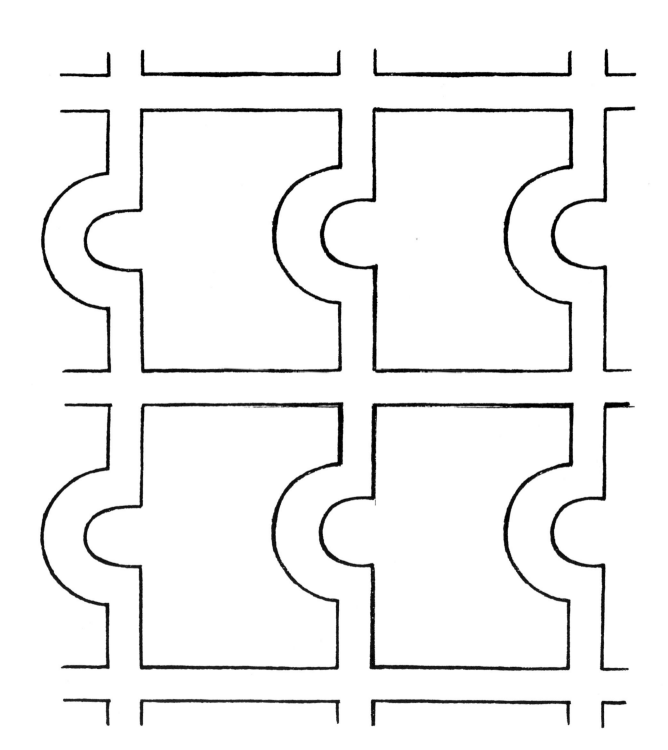

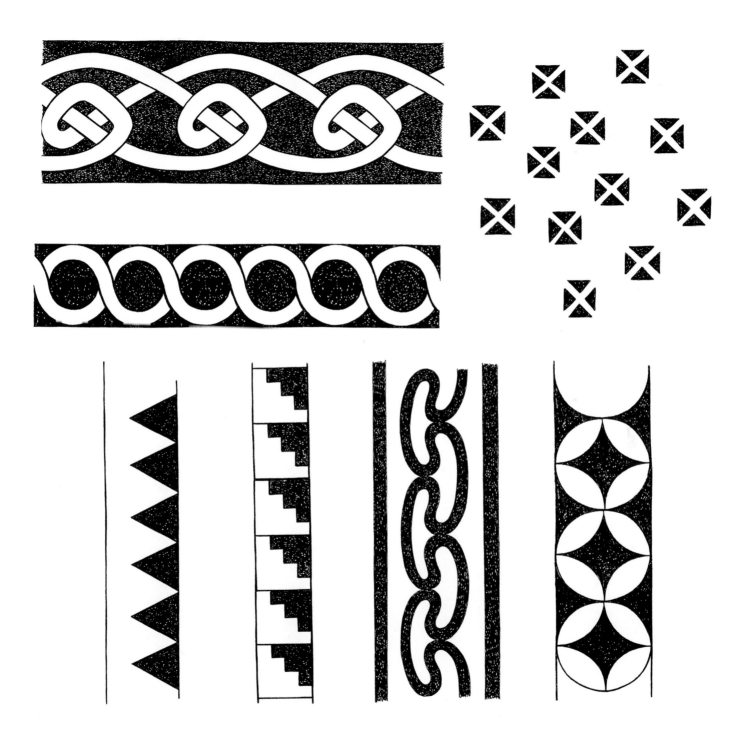

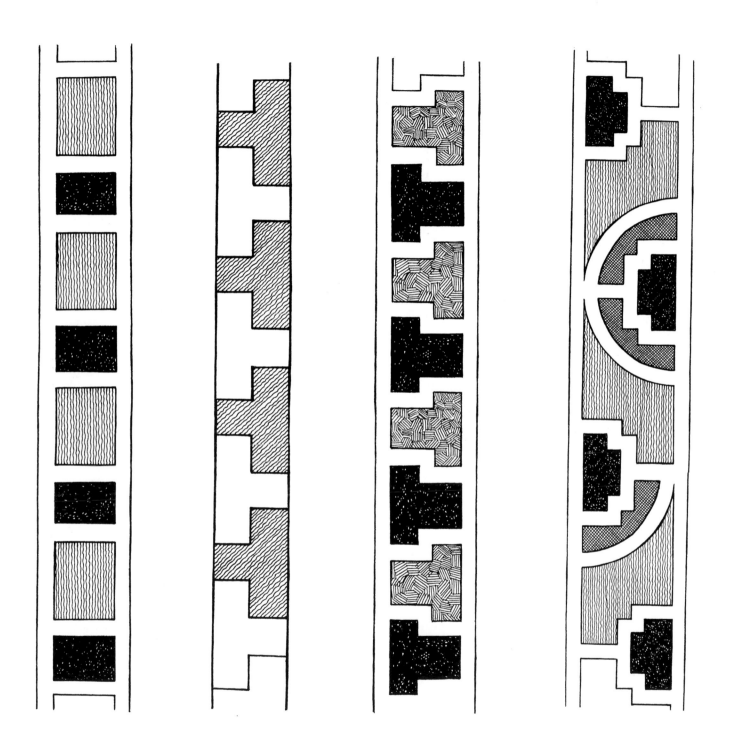

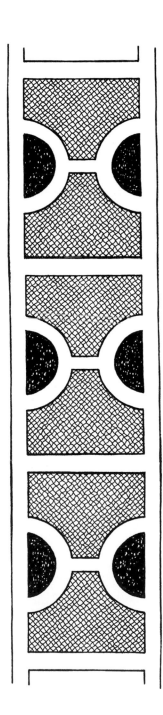
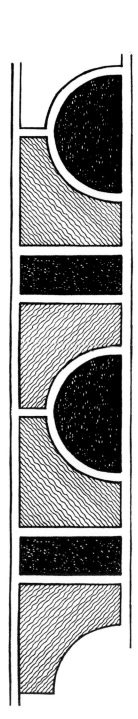
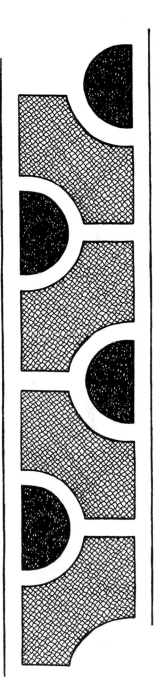

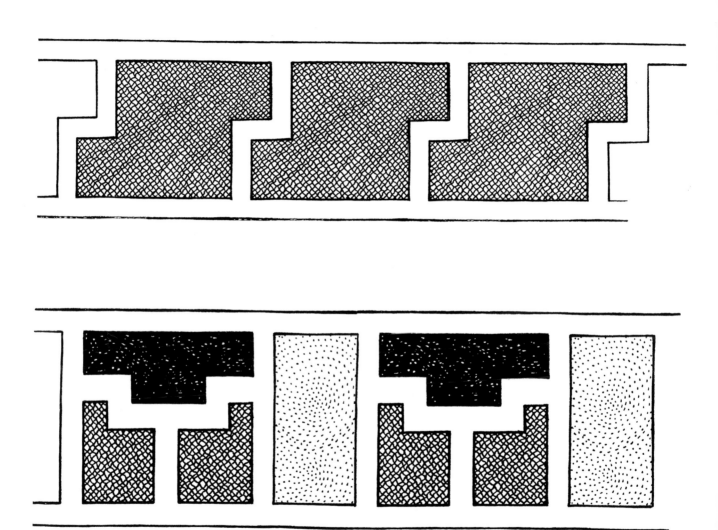

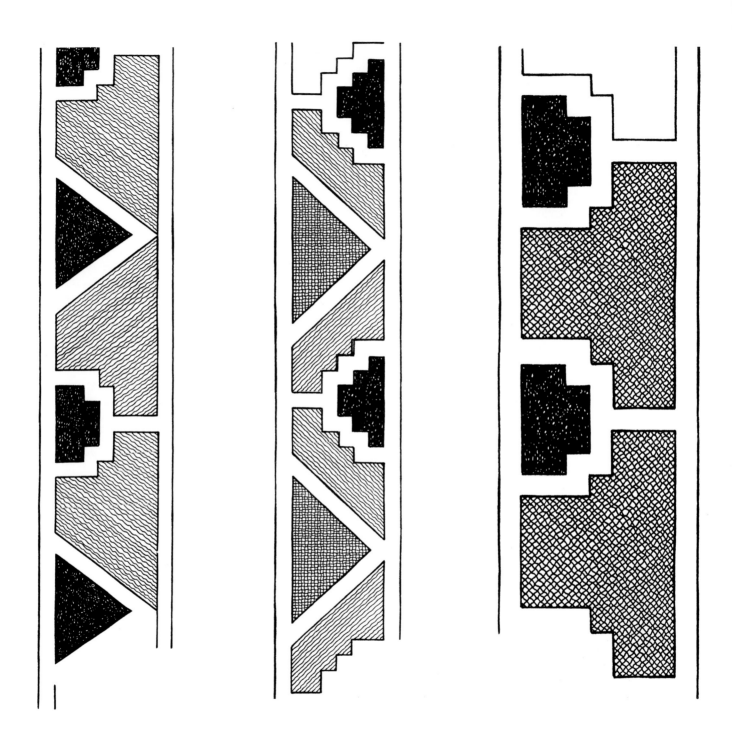

BYZANTINE

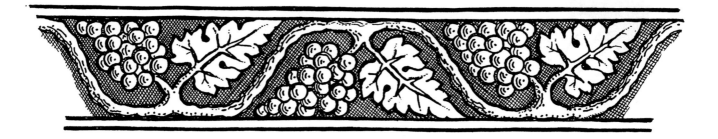

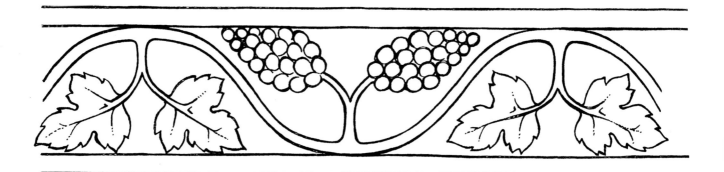

210 BYZANTINE

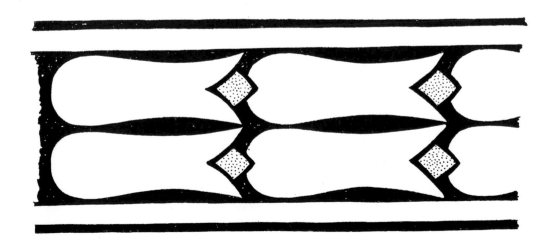

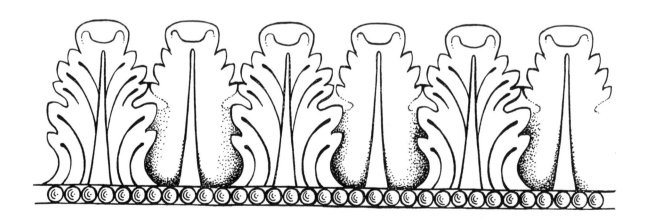

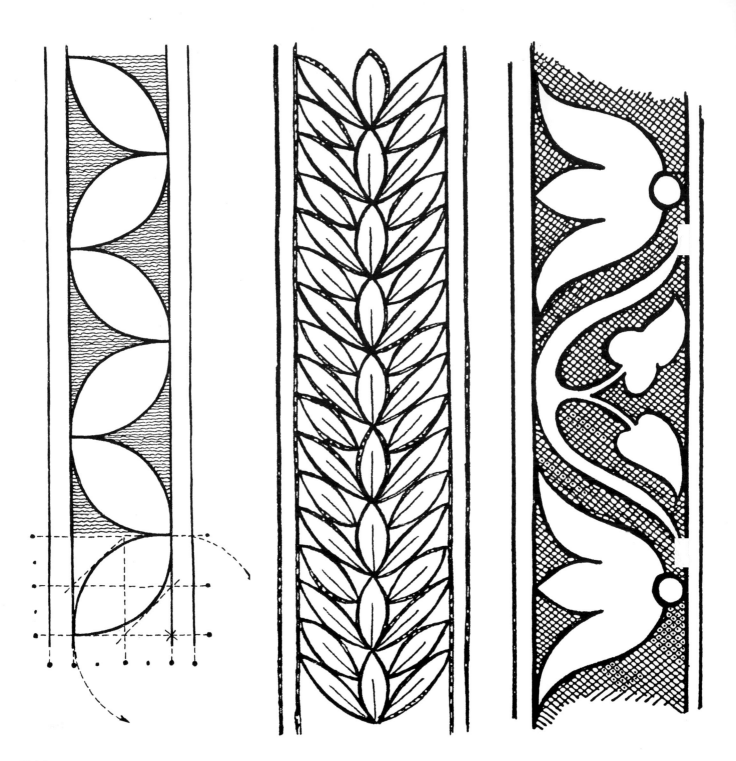

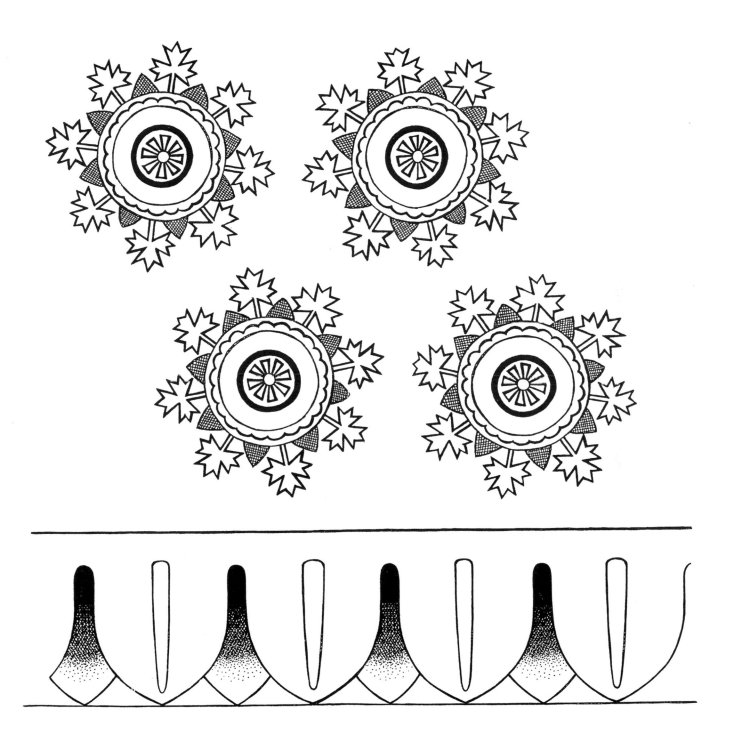

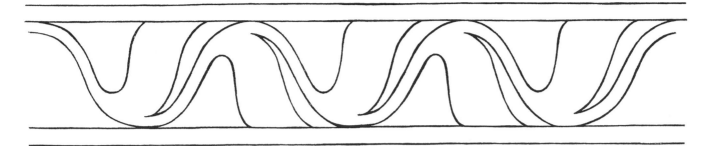

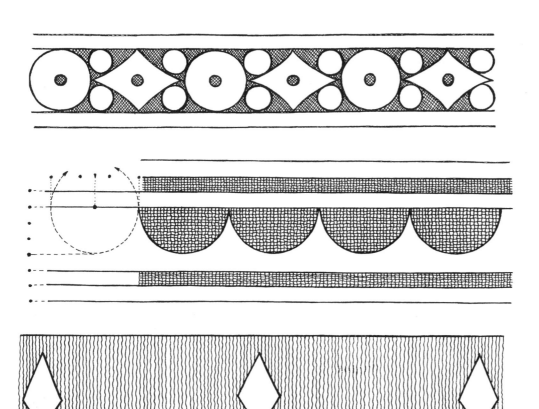

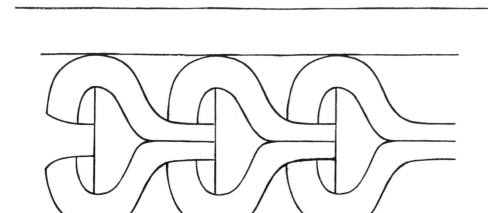

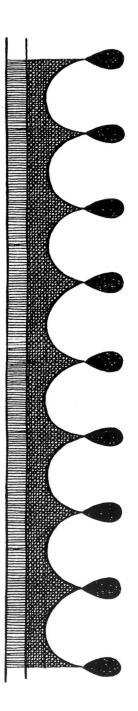

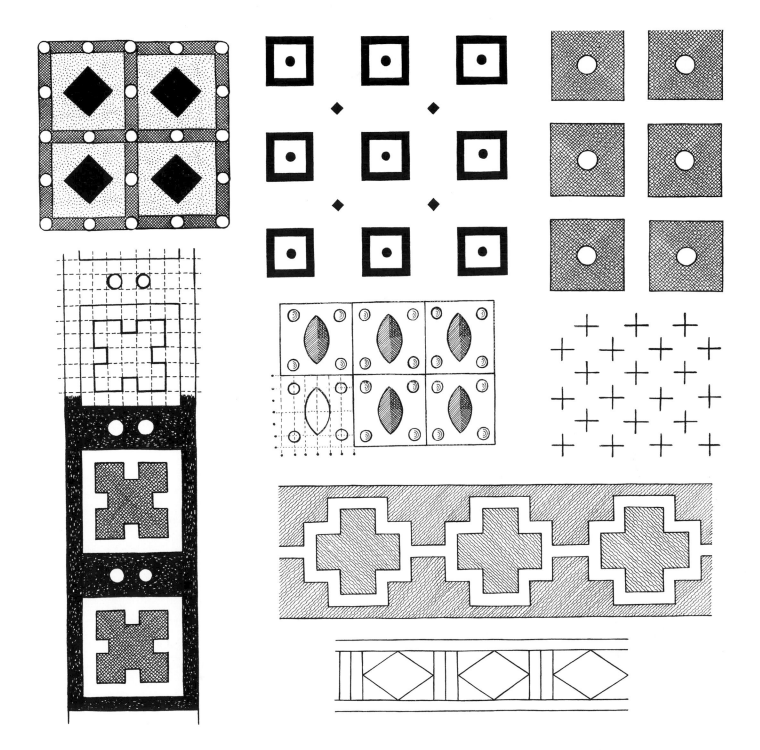

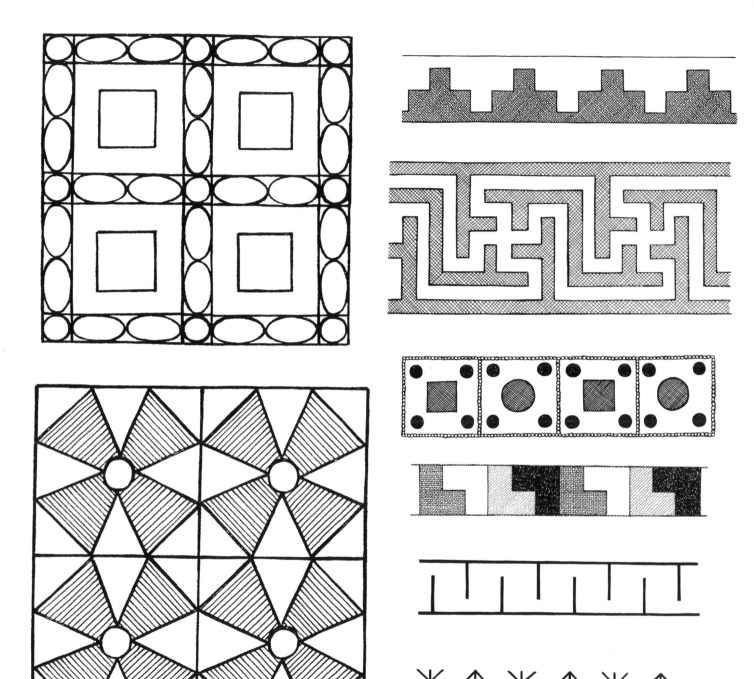

ROMANESQUE

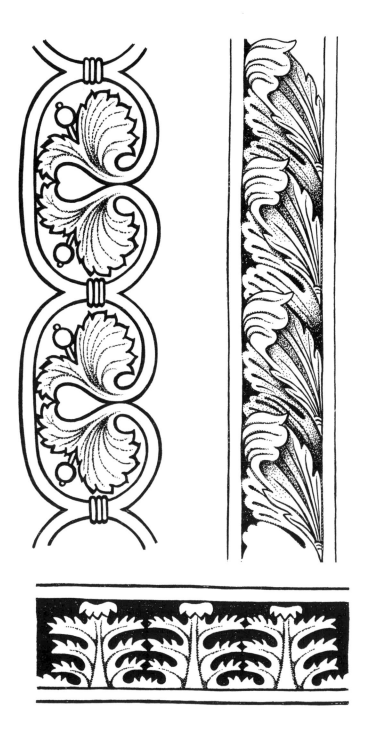

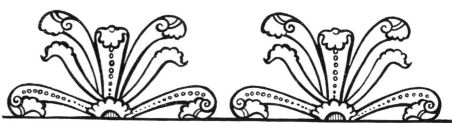

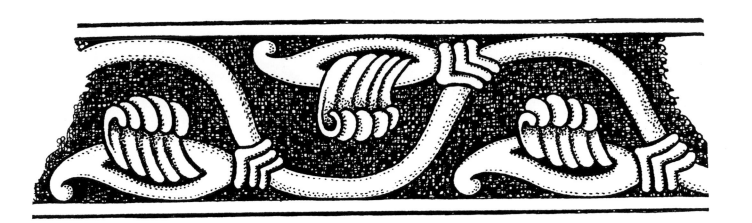

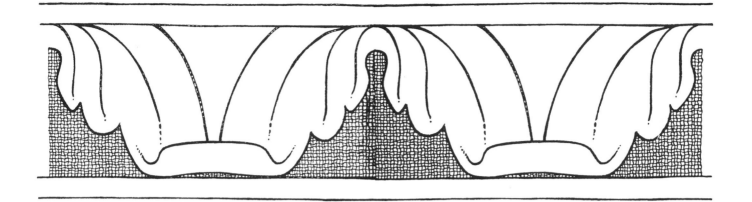

240 ROMANESQUE

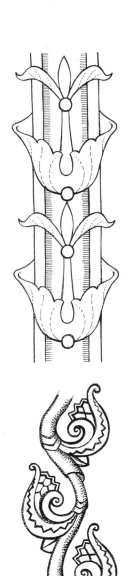

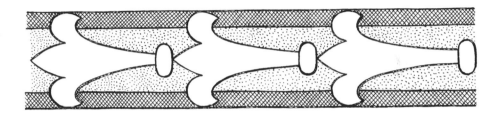

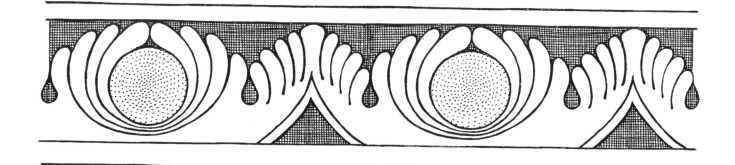

254 ROMANESQUE

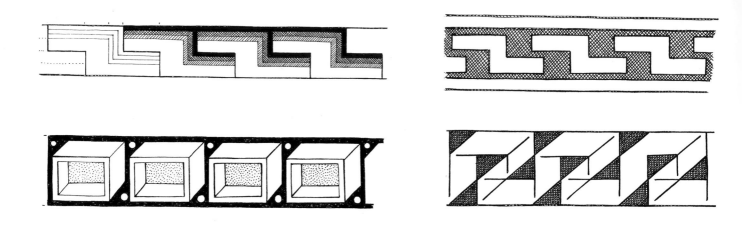

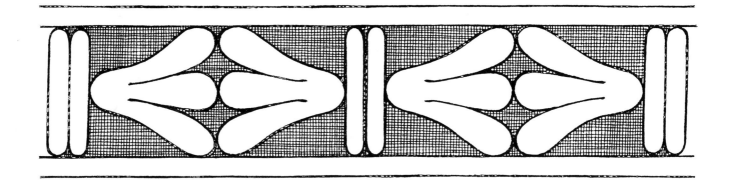

GOTHIC

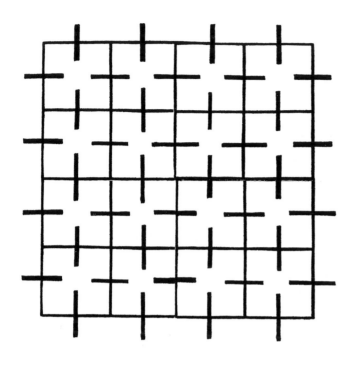

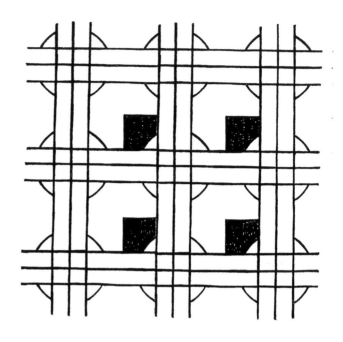

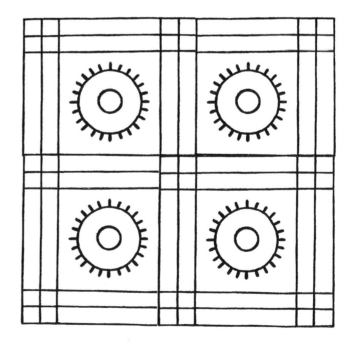

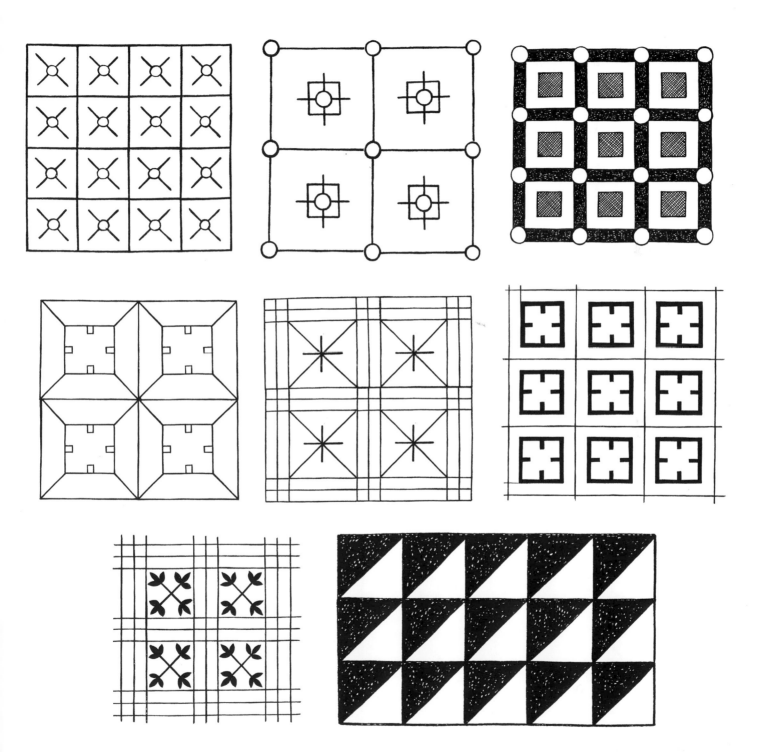

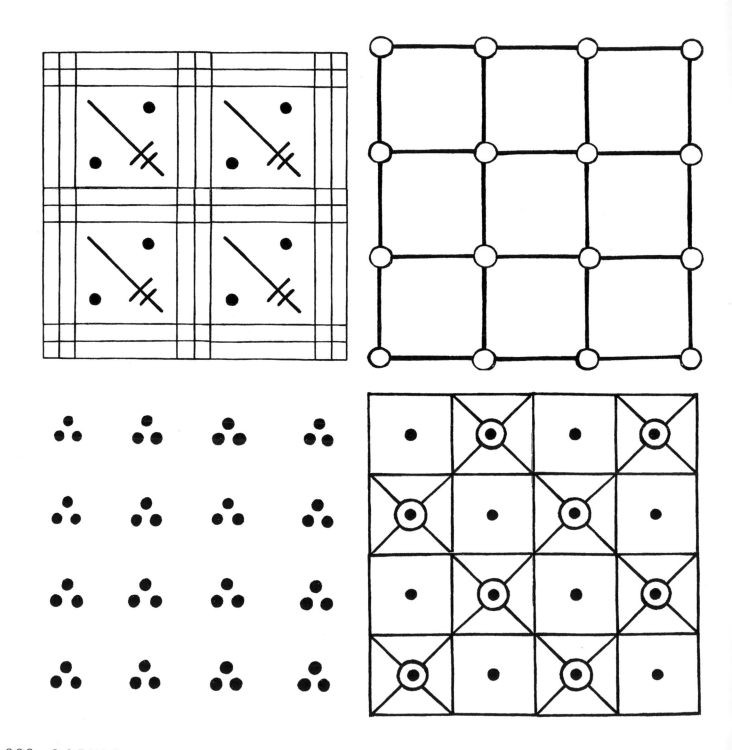

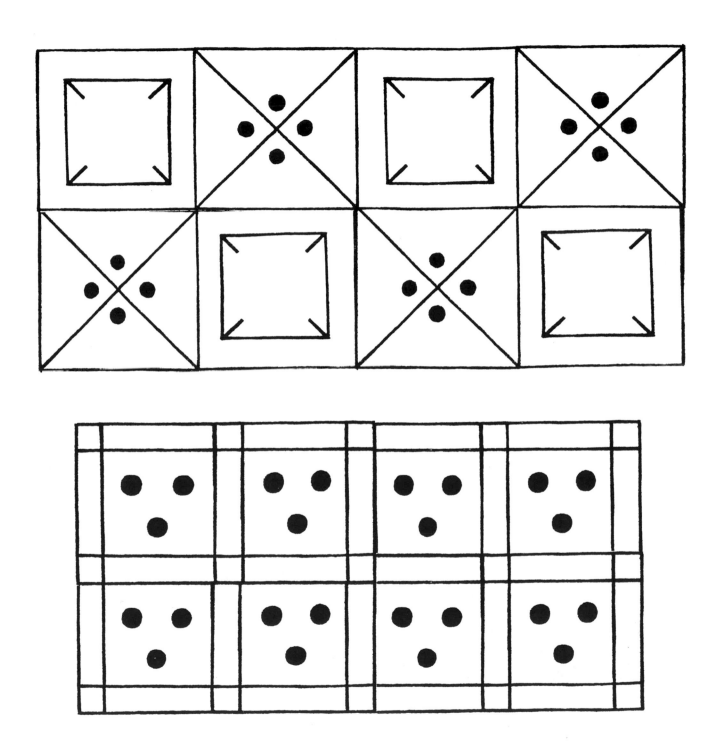

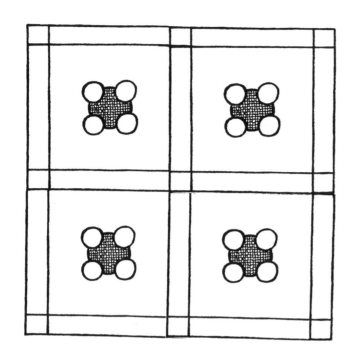

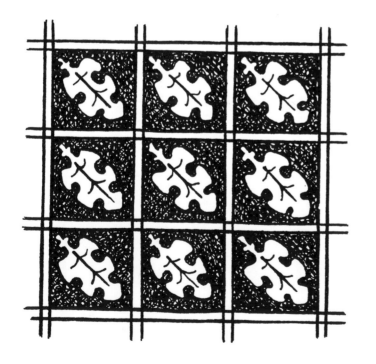

264 GOTHIC

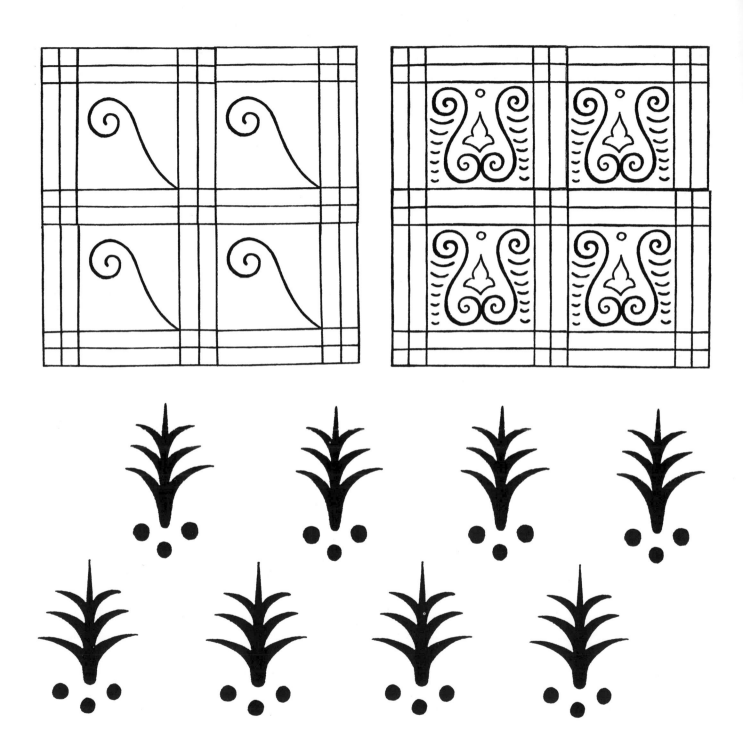

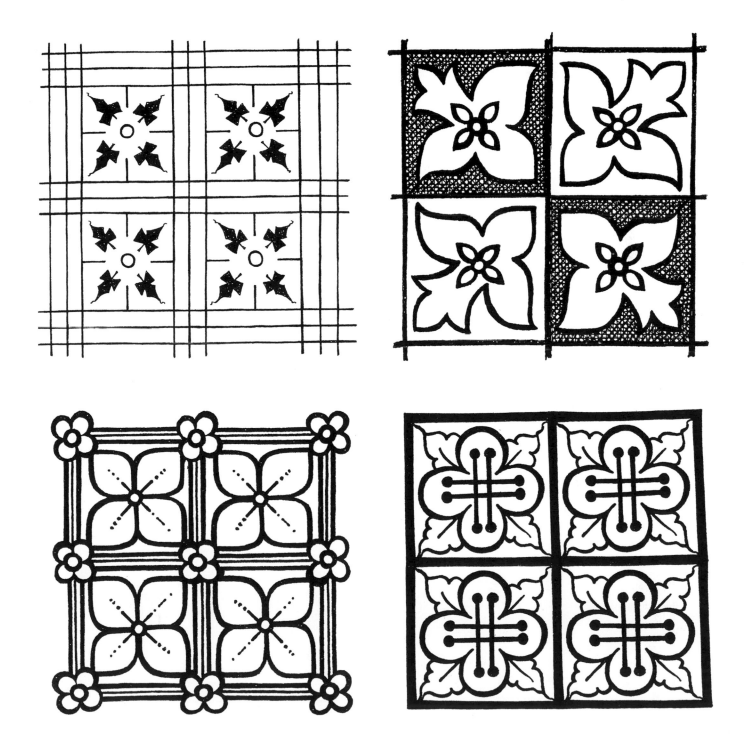

GOTHIC 269

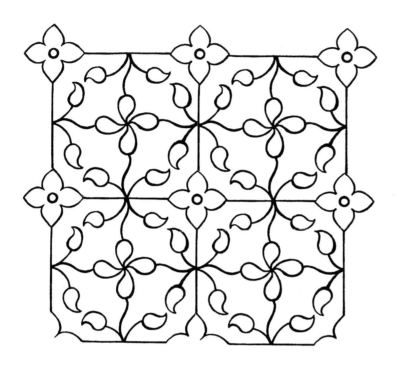

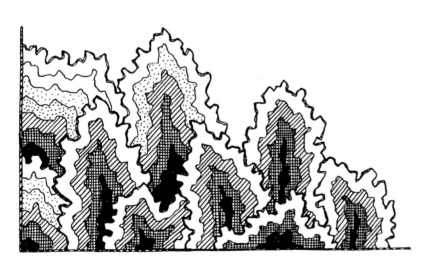

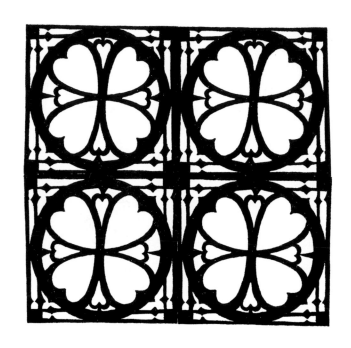

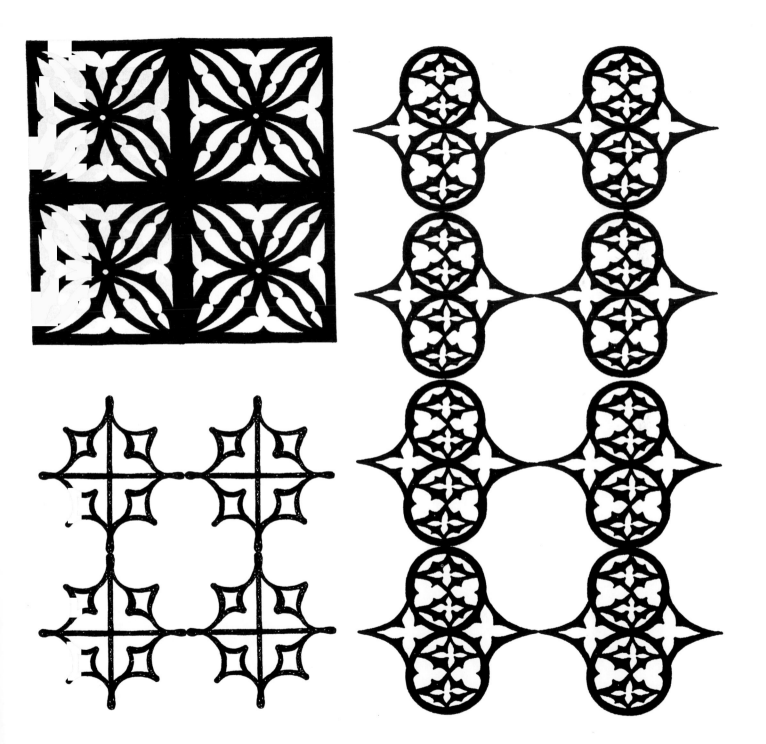

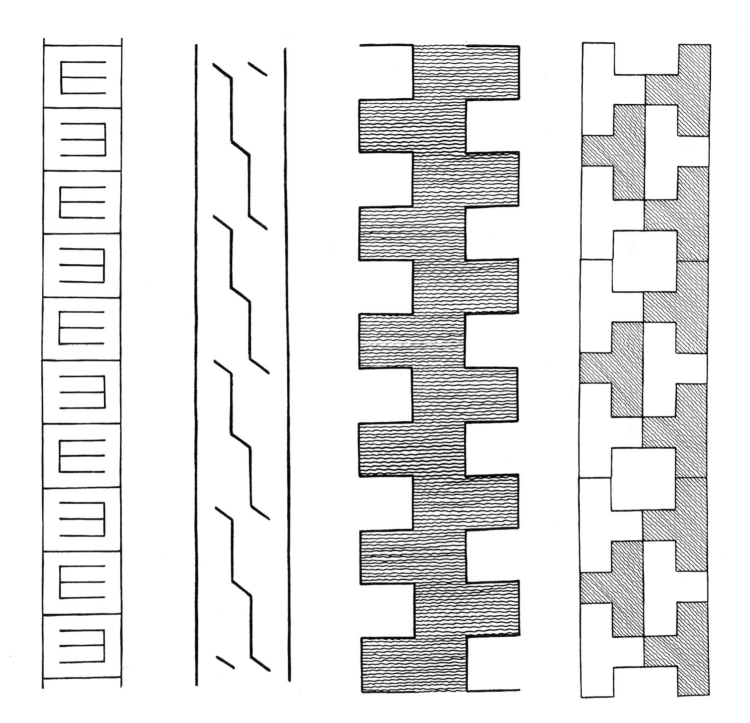

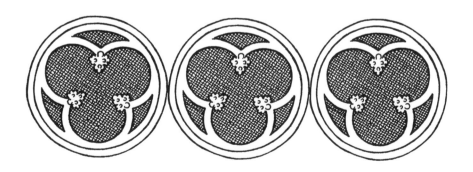

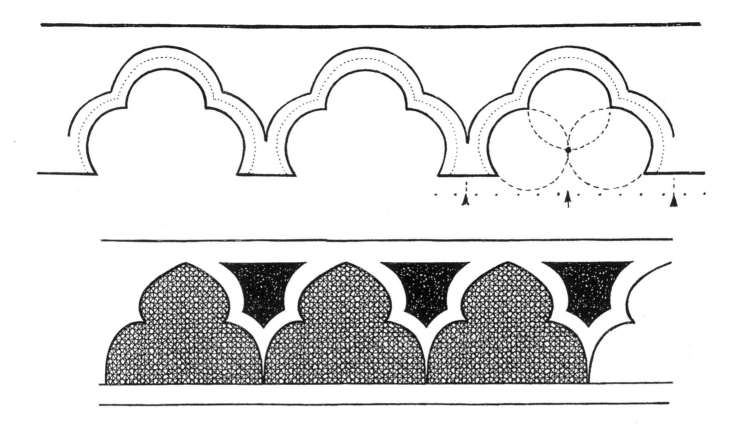

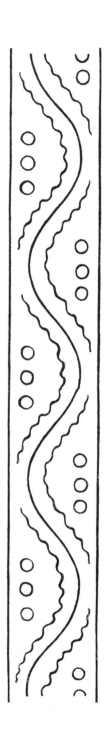

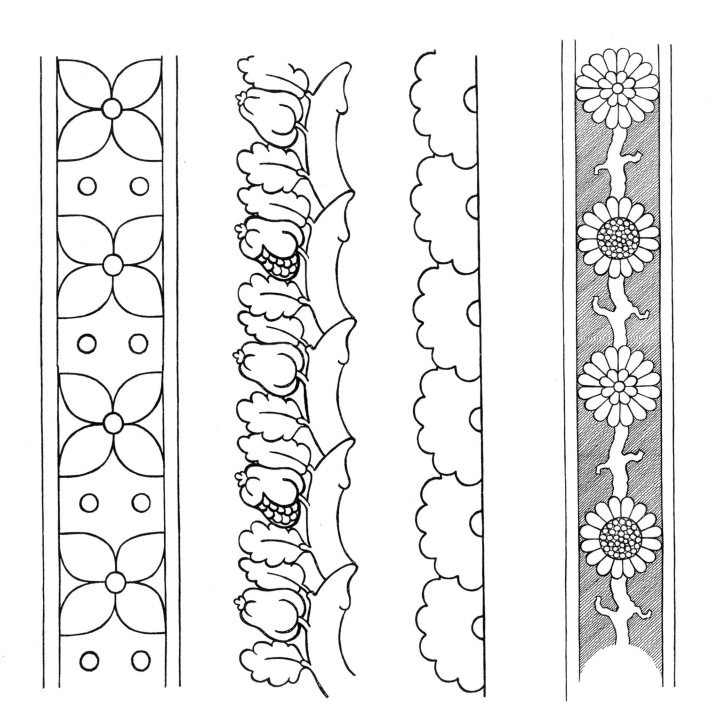

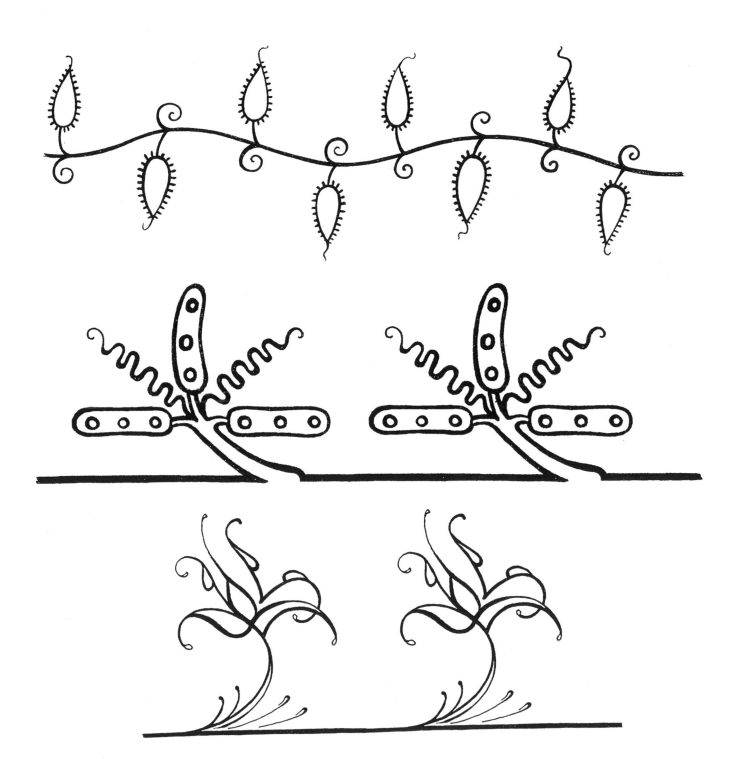

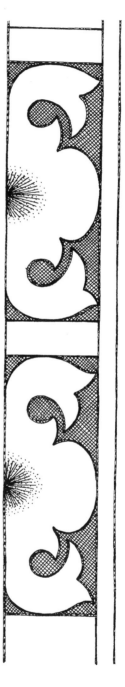

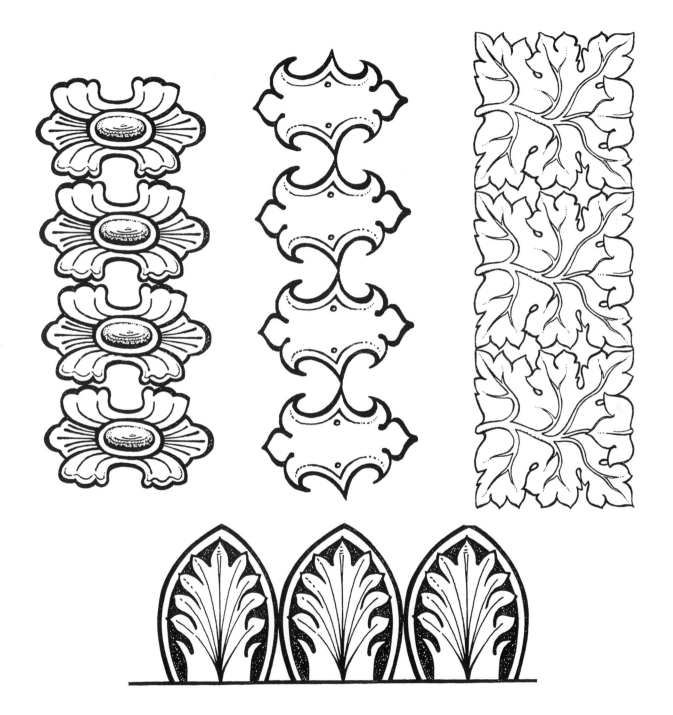

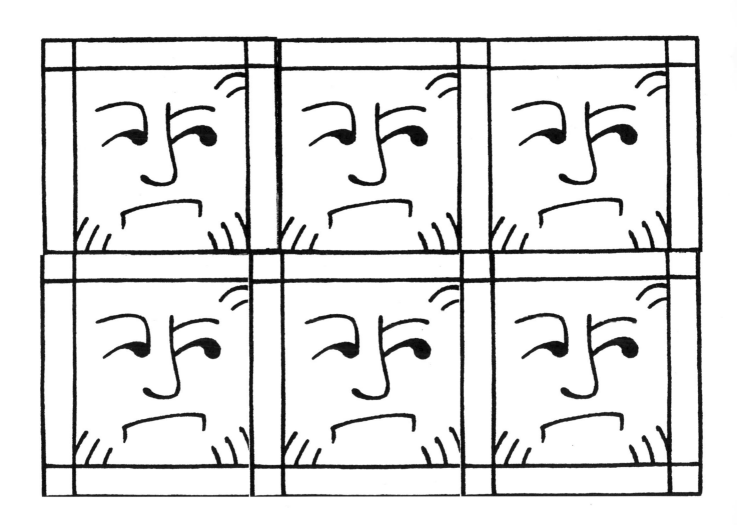

JAPANESE

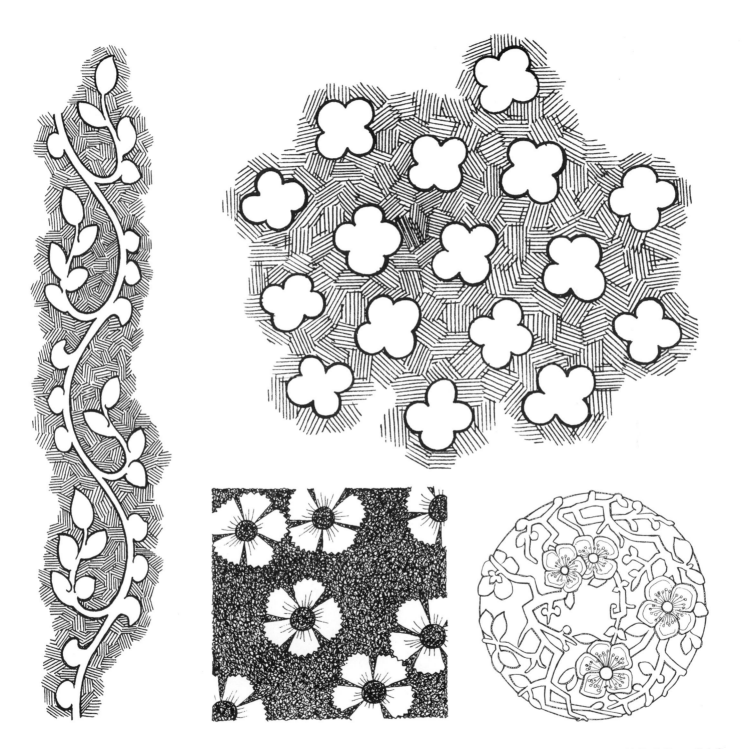

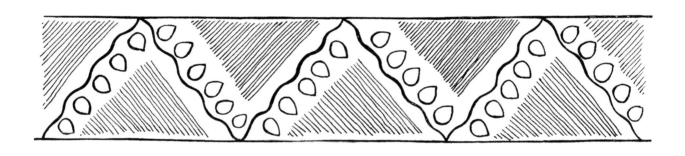

324 JAPANESE

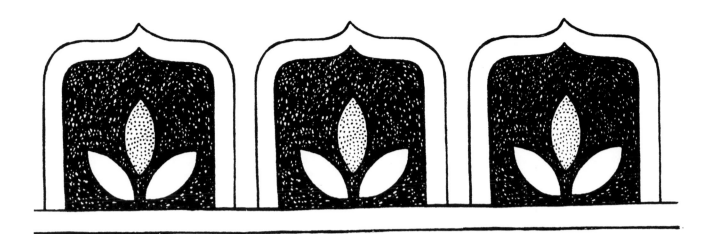

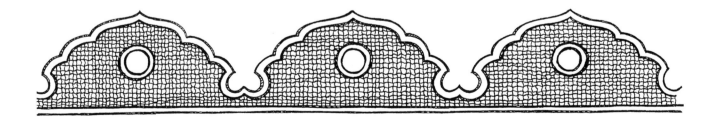

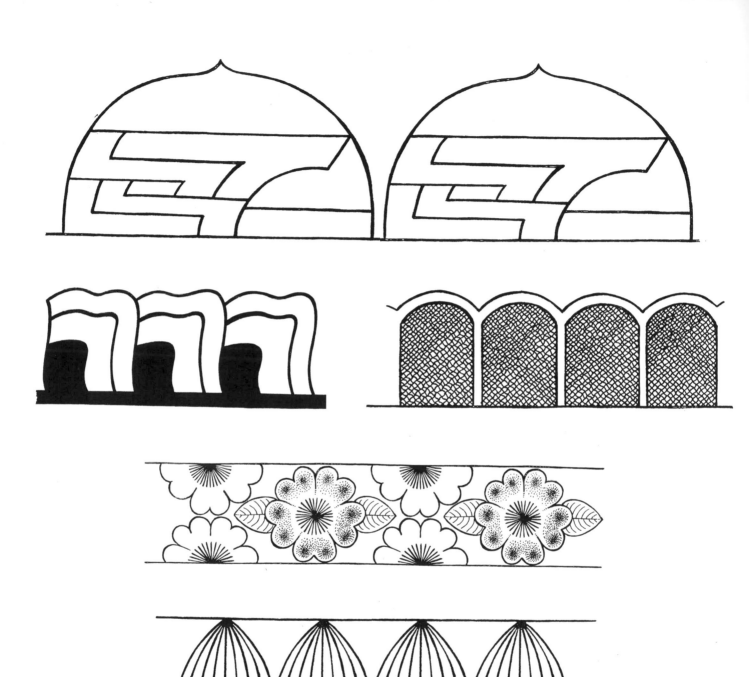

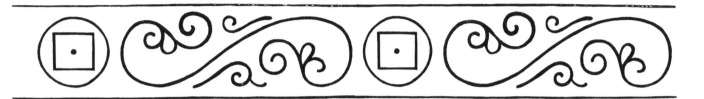

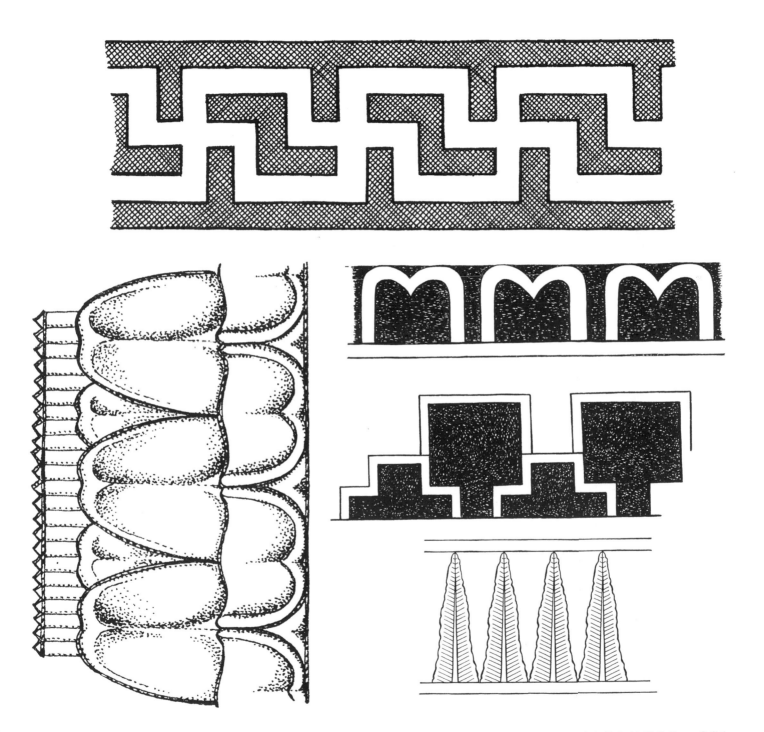

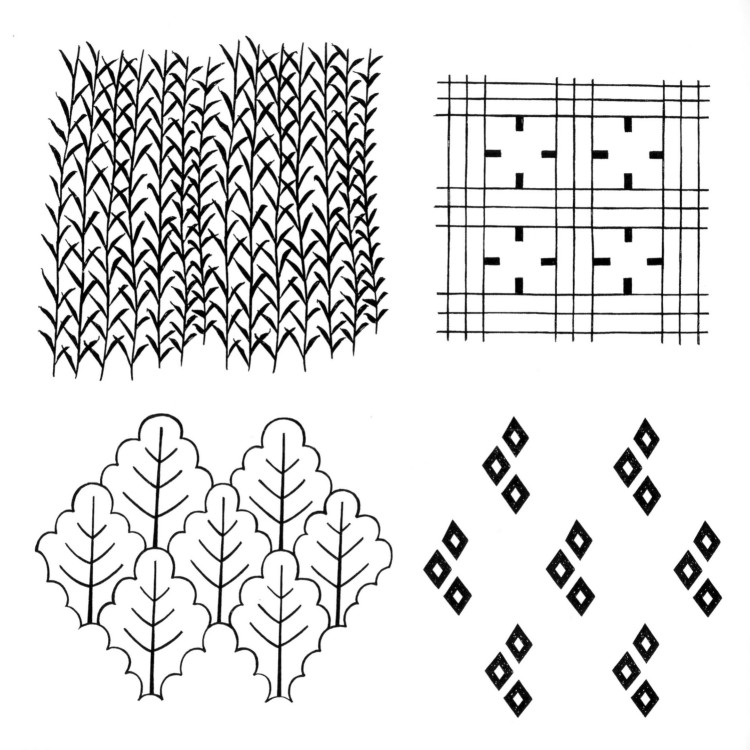

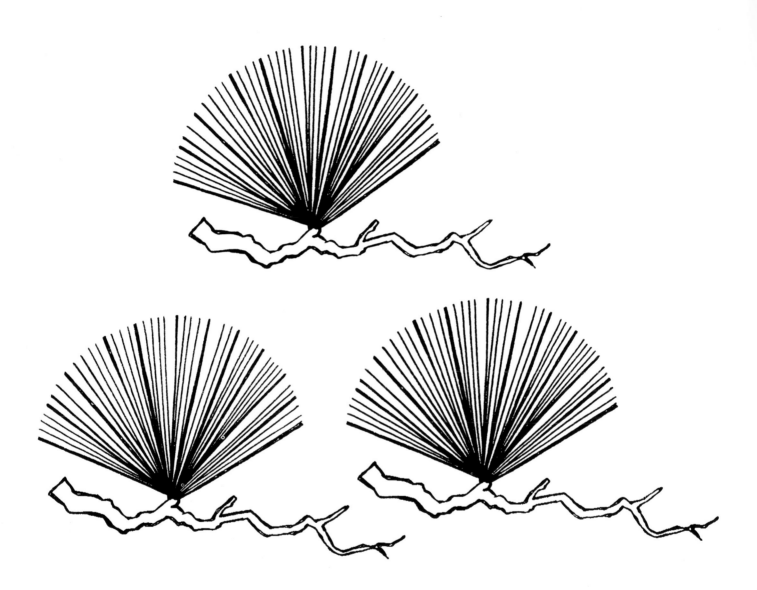

338 JAPANESE

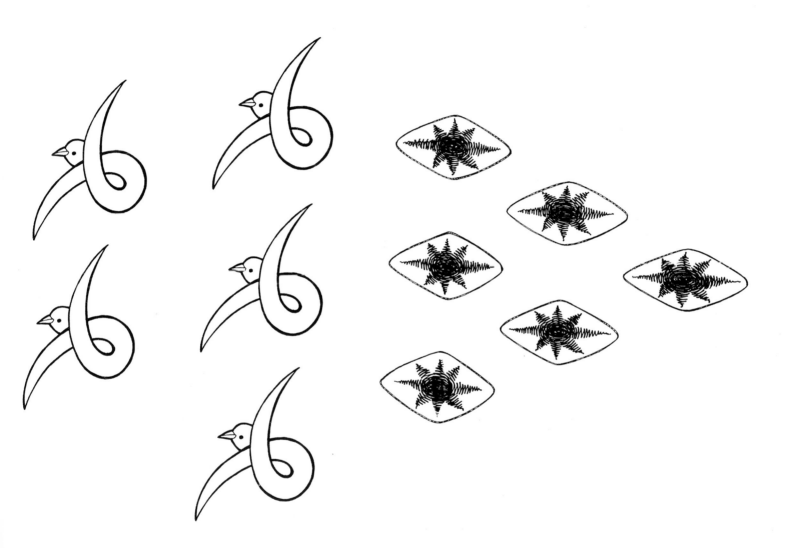

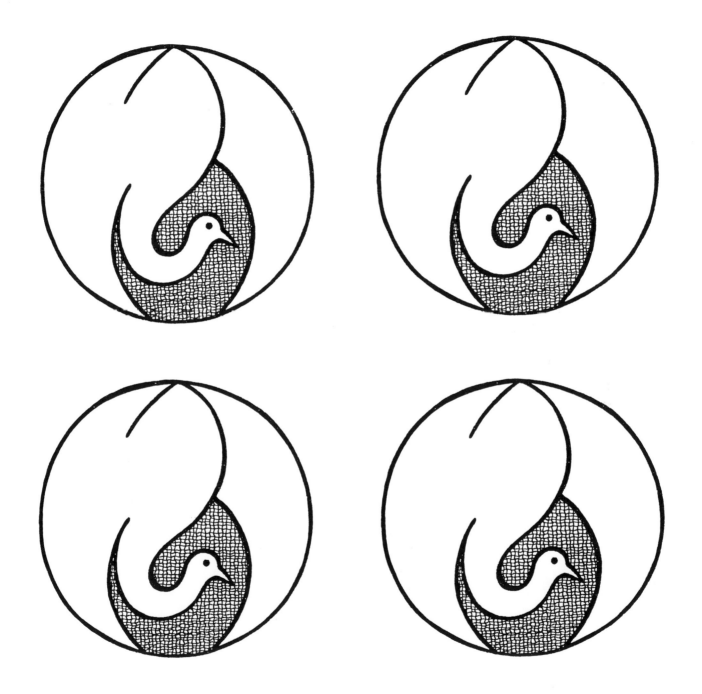

ART DECO

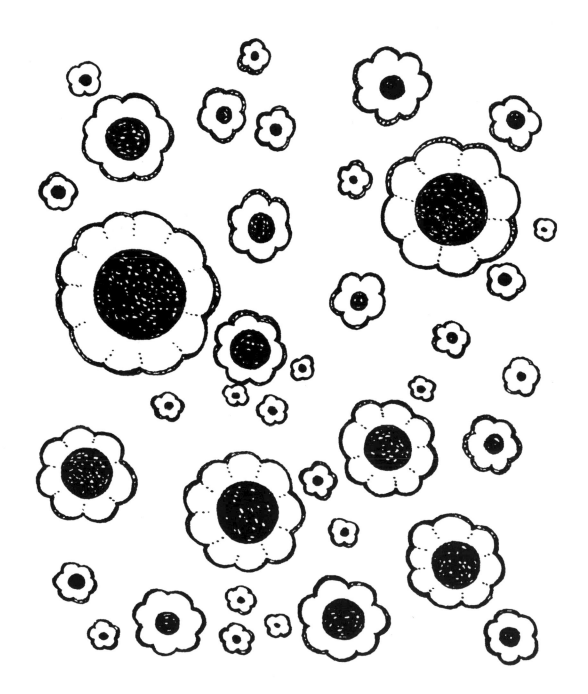

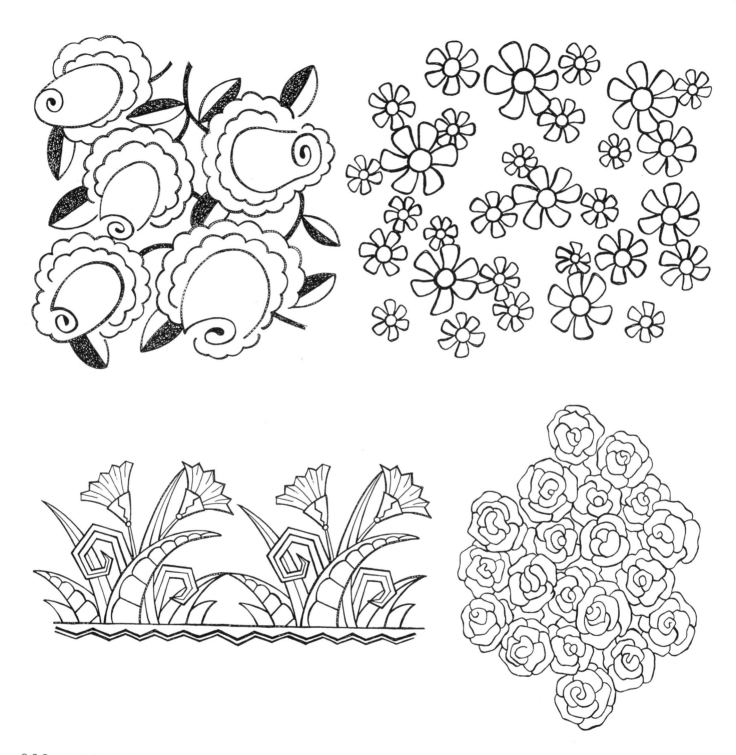

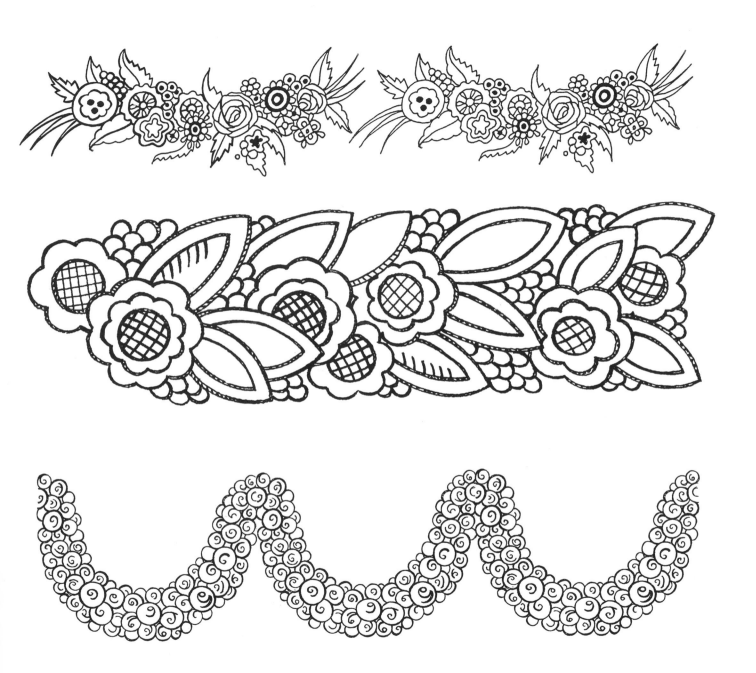

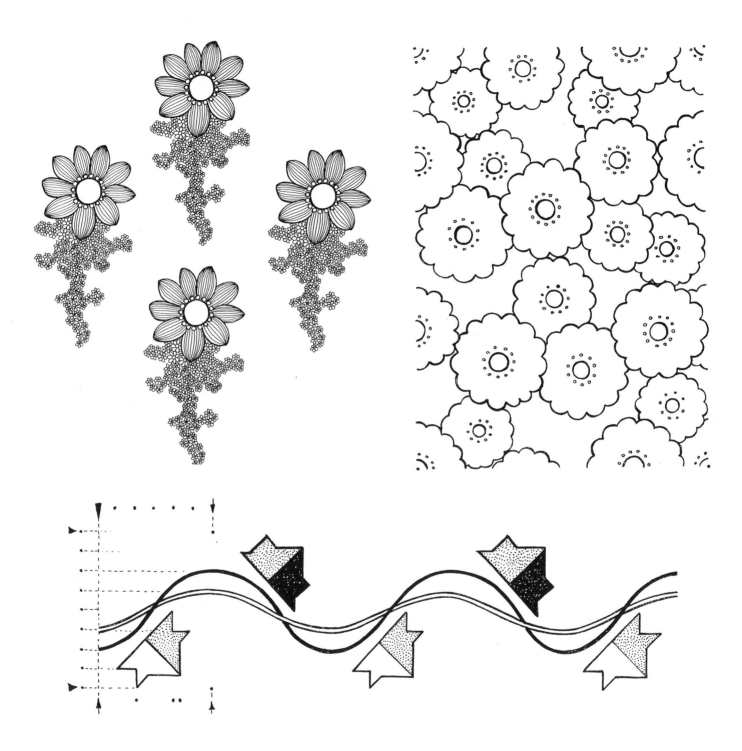

ART DECO 363

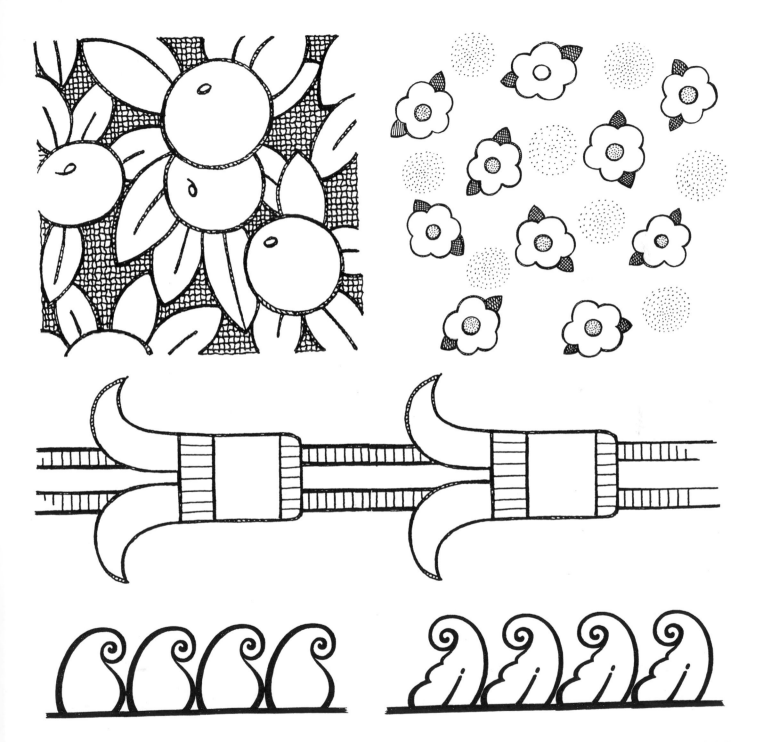

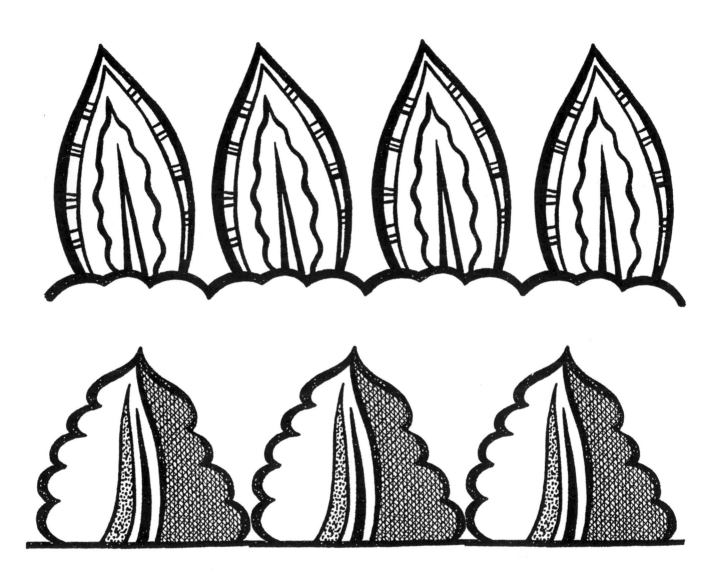

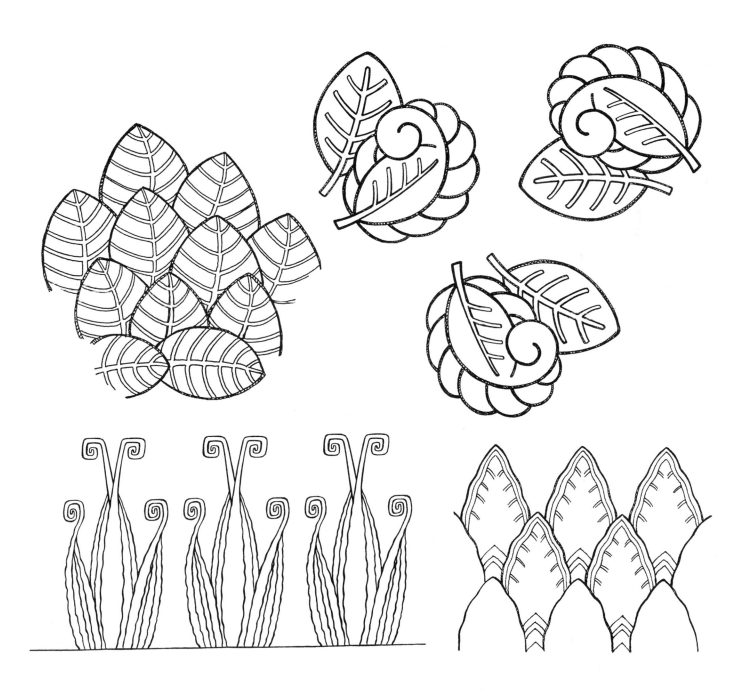

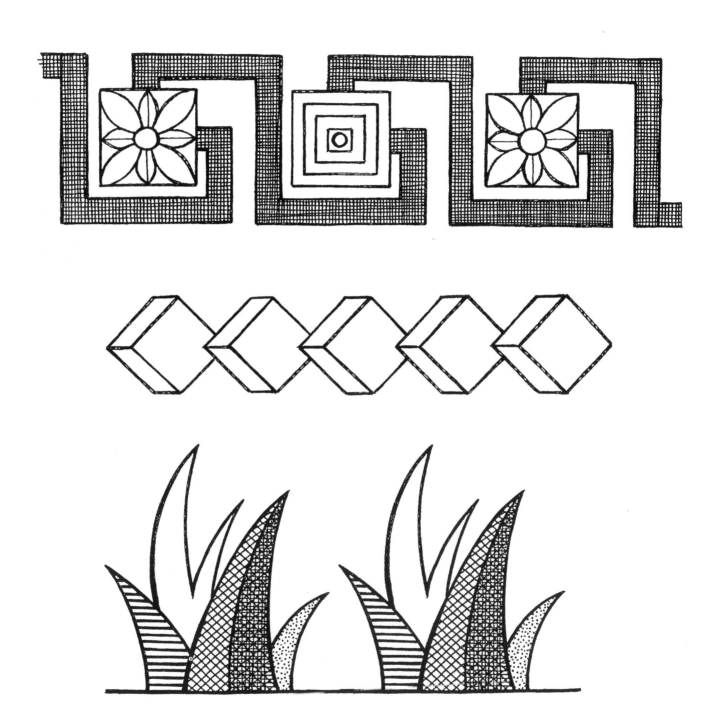

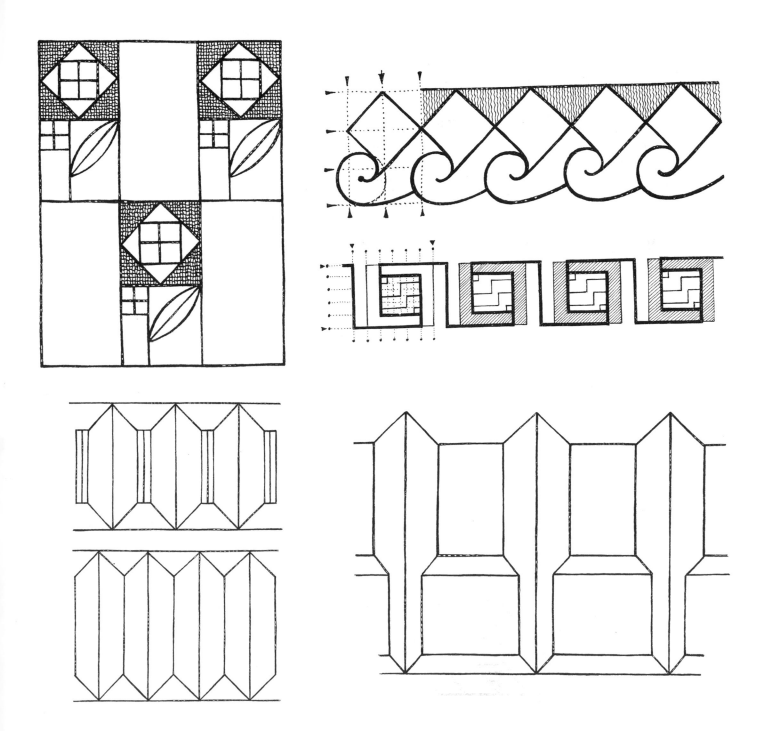

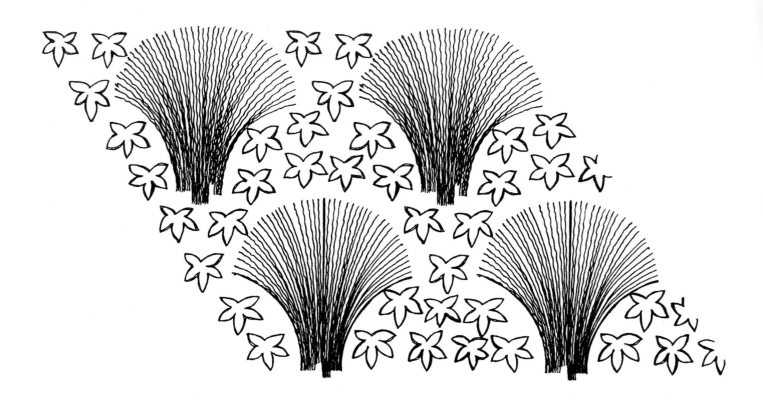

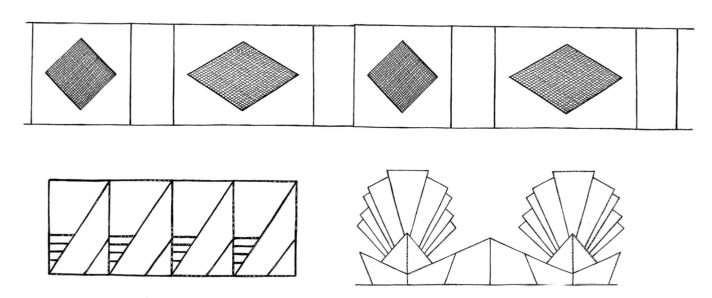

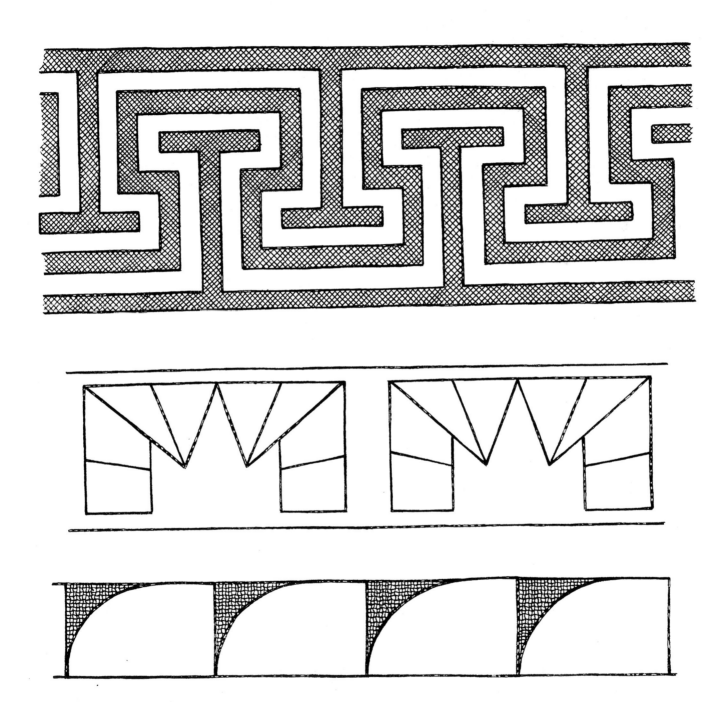

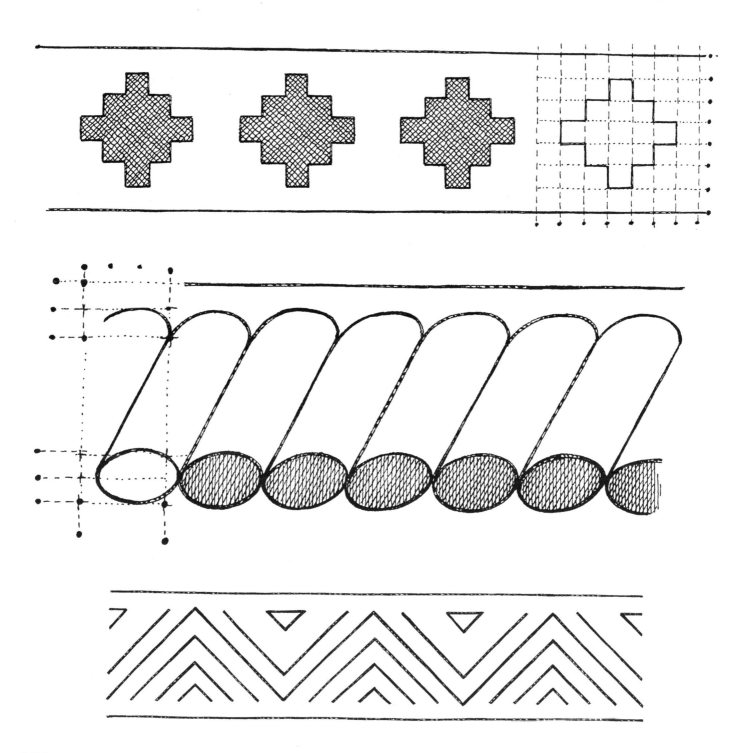

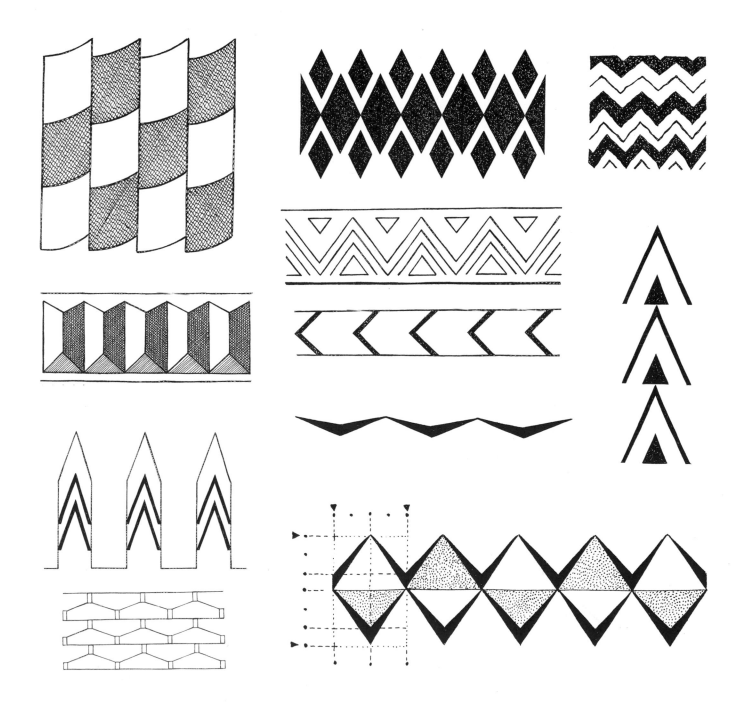

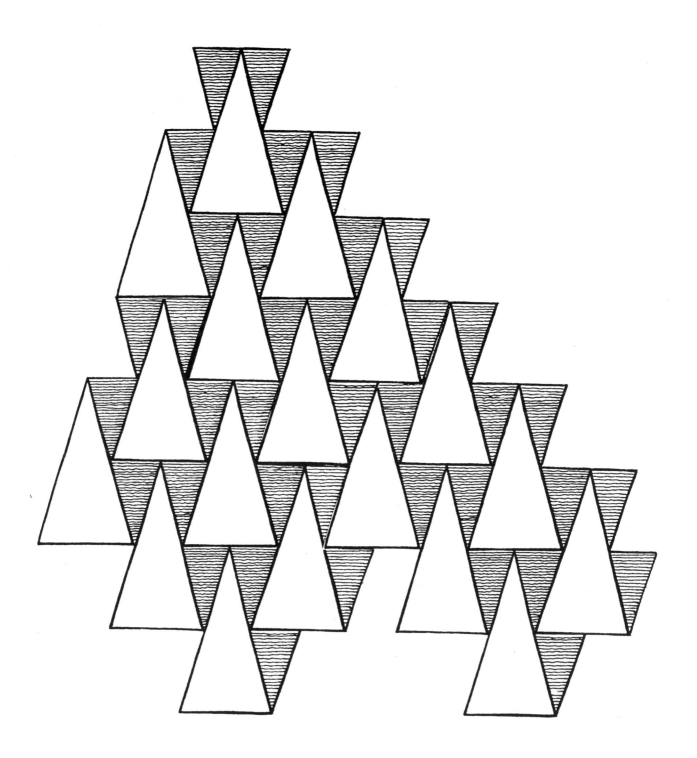

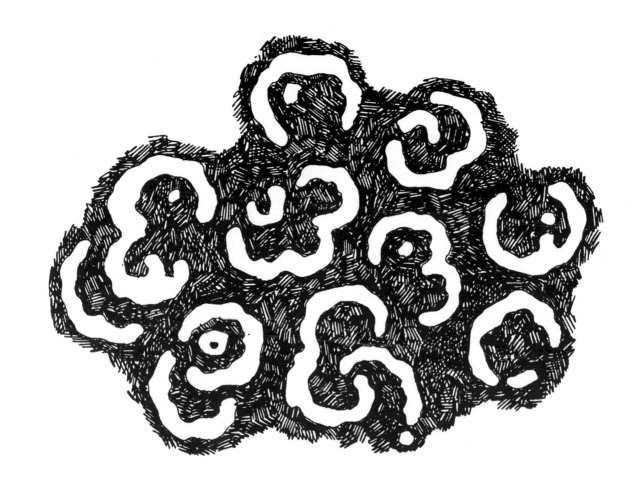

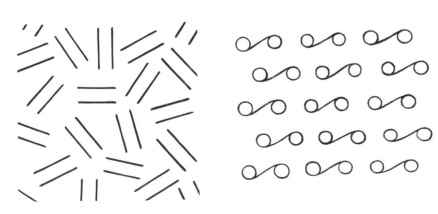

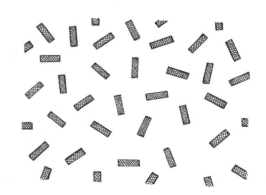

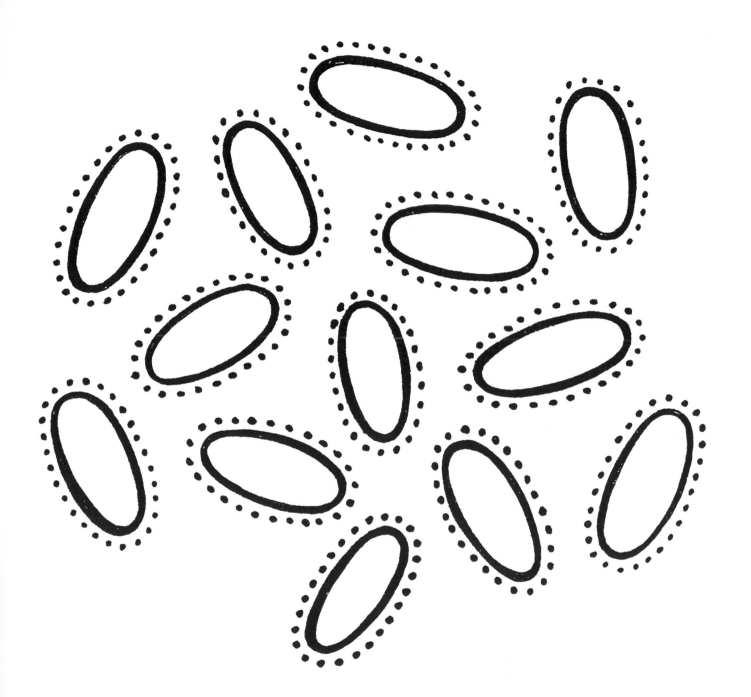